"Clarence Shuler is a godly man who has gaine[...] into depression from years of studying and teac[...] others, and from personally applying the word of God to his own heart and mind for decades."

—Stephen Kendrick,
Kendrick Brothers Productions; author, *The Battle Plan for Prayer*

"Wow, if you've ever struggled with depression, anxiety, or mental health issues, you have to read this book! Clarence takes you on a personal and very transparent journey through some of his darkest days. And throughout the book, he invites you into conversations with his counselor, Dr. Mo, which ultimately helped him find hope and light and can do the same for you."

—Jackie Bledsoe,
speaker and bestselling author of *The Seven Rings of Marriage*

"All of us can benefit from the quiet strength in Dr. Shuler's words. Just as he does at his powerful speaking events, Clarence delivers insight and guidance that will help you or someone you love walk from darkness into the light. You can—you will—find hope, purpose, love, and laughter again."

—Jay Payleitner,
national speaker and bestselling author of *The Next Verse*,
52 Things Kids Need from a Dad, and *What If God Wrote Your Bucket List?*

"This is Dr. Shuler's most important book. It is deeply personal, and plums the depths of mental and emotional suffering. This is not sermonic; it comes from the heart of a 'wounded healer.' I happily endorse this book."

—William Pannell,
professor emeritus, Fuller Theological Seminary

"Collaborating most creatively, Dr. Shuler with Dr. Gadson's commentary offer a path forward for each of us as we encounter seasons of discouragement, disappointments, and even depression. Whether it is a continuing crisis or a newly experienced trial, this book proposes a path forward. Beginning with understanding and progressing to realistic decision-making, a course is proposed that offers hope and growth. The assurance that God is with us in the midst of our struggles, bringing us 'treasures' there (Isaiah 45:3), is offered by Dr. Shuler in a calm and compassionate voice. Dr. Gadson asks a penetrating question in response to Dr. Shuler's writing: 'Can we sit in the dark for a while knowing God is with us?' This book is for each of us, because each of us will sooner or later face the kind of crisis that this writing is designed to address."

—Brian Teel,
senior vice president, Resource Exchange International

"Each chapter of Clarence Shuler's book *Finding Hope in a Dark Place* drips with a rare transparency. The way he and Dr. Mo use clinical answers and antidotes to respond to many of life's pains is like an ice pack on an aching muscle. In this age of alternate truths, cover ups, and excuses Clarence tells it like it is, like it was, and how it can be."

—Jerald January, Sr.,
senior pastor, Vernon Park Church of God, Lynwood, IL

"Dr. Shuler has walked the dark road of depression and openly invites readers into his story. Along with Dr. Mo, he shares indispensable wisdom for a journey toward healing and peace. The homework questions for each chapter give practical steps to allow God to lead you to brighter paths."

—Amy Roemer,
household manager, avid reader, and amateur theologian

"What a certain answer during uncertain times! This book bravely took on hard places and unspoken struggles. I appreciate the tenderness of the authors as they gave open access to vulnerable conversations that not only validate and equip but give direction and hope. Give yourself grace and read this to find practical ways to identify, confront, and walk through your own tough spaces! You will get clarity of the 'What' and concrete ways in the 'How.' This is definitely your next step!"

—Shundria Riddick, MA, LPC,
therapist; speaker; author, *Married for Five Minutes:*
Hope for Living Inside Real Marriages

"*Finding Hope in a Dark Place* provides a brave, honest, and insightful look at depression through the lens of a man and his therapist friend. In addition to hard-earned wisdom and clinical expertise, Clarence and Dr. Monique have gifted us a beautiful example of how the simple yet often overlooked art of authentic connection brings powerful healing into dark places."

—Dr. Alison Cook,
author of *The Best of You* and *Boundaries for Your Soul*

"Dr. Shuler's *Finding Hope in a Dark Place* takes us on an epic journey and combines real life stories that translate powerful, evidence-based strategies to help us cope with loneliness, depression, and anxiety in our everyday lives. Comprehensive yet engaging from both personal and clinical perspectives, it is brilliantly written and gives practical principles on how to heal with the grace of God. This life-changing book is a must-read for all, especially those engaged in ministry."

—Dr. H. Malcolm Newton,
president, Urban Tikkun Center, Denver Institute of Urban Studies

"Romans 5:3–4 are two of my favorite verses: 'Not only that, but we rejoice in our sufferings, knowing that suffering produces endurance, and endurance produces character, and character produces hope' (ESV). If you know Clarence, he is a man of great character and in *Finding Hope in a Dark Place*, Clarence shares personally about the suffering of depression which he endured with God's help, his family, his friends, and yes, his therapist. Oftentimes we believe that depression and anxiety are a sign of weakness, yet through great insight, wise counsel, and Clarence's real-life experience–and along with the great support of Dr. Mo—we learn suffering and healing are parts of life to be embraced. A 'dark place' is really a place where light makes all the difference. Of course, be prepared to be challenged and changed."

—Wayne R Connell,
coauthor of *But You LOOK Good: How to Encourage and Understand People Living with Illness and Pain* and *Not By Sight: Ministering to Believers Living with Illness and Pain*; CEO and founder of the Invisible Disabilities Association

"Grabbing this book is like grabbing a flashlight when life is pitch black. As Clarence and Dr. Mo walk you through their real-life journey to his recovery, you too can find your way through the darkness and into the light of hope. Their book is a field guide for your feelings—helping you filter your emotions, process your pain points, and chart your own path to healing and restoration."

—Jenée V. Giles-Hamilton,
TV writer

FINDING HOPE IN A DARK PLACE

Facing Loneliness, Depression, and Anxiety with the Power of Grace

FINDING HOPE IN A DARK PLACE

Facing Loneliness, Depression, and Anxiety with the Power of Grace

CLARENCE SHULER

WITH **MONIQUE S. GADSON, PhD, LPC**

KIRKDALE PRESS

Finding Hope in a Dark Place: Facing Loneliness, Depression, and Anxiety with the Power of Grace

Copyright 2022 Clarence Shuler and Monique S. Gadson

Kirkdale Press, 1313 Commercial St., Bellingham, WA 98225
LexhamPress.com/Kirkdale-Press

Print ISBN 9781683596356
Digital ISBN 978-1683596363
Library of Congress Control Number 2022941651

Kirkdale Editorial: Deborah Keiser, Kelsey Matthews, Elizabeth Vince, Mandi Newell
Cover Design: Joshua Hunt, Brittany Schrock
Typesetting: Justin Marr

This book is dedicated to anyone who is or has struggled with darkness depression or mental health issue and does not feel good about his or herself. It is also for all those who love those who are wrestling with being in a dark place.

—C. S.

To those who weep, who worry, who wait—may you experience the sufficiency found in the grace of God. I pray your hearts and minds be guarded by the Comforter, especially during the dark times in life.

—M. G.

CONTENTS

WHEN YOU'RE IN A DARK PLACE

FINDING HOPE

Practicing New Ways of Being

FOREWORD

GARY CHAPMAN

As humans, we are all greatly influenced by our past and present circumstances. This influence may be positive or negative. For those who have had negative experiences in their past, the memories tend to follow us, hiding in the shadows. When our present circumstances turn negative, the memories of the past seem to pounce on us, leading us to a dark place where hope seems to take flight. Have you been there? Are you presently in a dark place? If so, this book is for you.

The challenge is to acknowledge our painful circumstances without allowing them to control our behavior. To quote from the book; "Don't let the pain of your past punish your present, paralyze your future, and pervert your purpose because you have a godly destiny." The authors fully acknowledge that Christians may experience loneliness, depression, and anxiety. However, Christians have One who walks with them through the dark places. The God who walks with us often uses fellow pilgrims like pastors, counselors, and friends to express his love and assure us that we are not alone.

One of the unique aspects of this book is that in every chapter you will hear the voice of Clarence Shuler, who has walked in and out of dark places throughout his life, and Monique Gadson a trained Christian counselor whom God has used to help him not to remain in those dark places.

God will not only walk with us but wants to use our troubled seasons to help others. Paul, the apostle once said: "He comforts us in all our troubles so that we can comfort others. When they are troubled, we will be able to give them the same comfort God has given us. For the more we suffer for Christ, the more God will shower us with his comfort through Christ" (2 Corinthians 1:4–5 NLT). Thus Clarence says, "Sometimes God may allow us to suffer not just for our sake, but so that we may know how to help others who suffer after we've come out of our dark place. So our being in our dark place is not just about us."

In a very real sense, this book is an effort to help those who are struggling learn from the experience of Clarence. He is now an author, speaker, mentor, and pastoral counselor who has invested his life in helping others. Monique is doing the same by sharing what she has learned through the years as a counselor of those who are experiencing difficult mental, emotional, and spiritual struggles.

If you or a friend of yours is in a dark place, this book offers guidance. Clarence is very vulnerable in sharing his own struggles, and Monique was very empathetic with him and with the reader. Her practical suggestions are biblically based and point to Christ who is our constant friend and companion.

As you read, remember the words of Jesus: "Come to me all you who are weary and burdened, and I will give you rest. Take my yoke upon you and learn from me, for I am gentle and humble in heart, and you will find rest for your souls. For my yoke is easy and my burden is light" (Matthew 11:28–30 NIV). When, in our stress we join with him, we have a divine companion who will never leave us or forsake us.

WILL YOU JOIN ME ON
THIS JOURNEY?

Have you ever felt that you were in a dark place? If so, did you ask yourself how you got there? Was it due to some feelings of anxiety, inadequacy, rejection, or loneliness, or a situation like a divorce, a miscarriage, not being popular, or experiencing aging issues?

We can find ourselves in a dark place for a variety of reasons. Possibly you struggle with not being popular; you feel like you don't have any friends or you don't have enough friends. Or maybe you feel you don't have the *right* friends, possibly resulting in your not feeling good about who you are. Transitioning from middle school to high school or college or from college to what is called "the real world" may create a dark place for you because of the uncertainly of so many things.

The coronavirus impacted the entire world! Did it make you fearful for your future? Did you struggle to experience peace during the uncertainty of that virus? The various new strands of the virus probably didn't make you feel any better. This has created anxiety for some.

Maybe aging is an issue. You may have concerns because it seems your body is letting you down. No longer can you do the things physically that you used to do well. And this is affecting how you feel about yourself. Possibly, you are losing your independence.

You are now depending more and more on family and friends, or you're living in some form of assisted living. Your mind is still sharp, but those caring for you no longer recognize or appreciate it like they formerly did. Or your ability to remember has become a point of frustration for you. Perhaps you'll retire soon, and society—at least American society—doesn't seem to value your maturity and wisdom, and your future is more uncertain than ever. All of this may cause you to devalue yourself.

It is not uncommon for those in their sixties to begin focusing on death because losing their peers becomes more and more common. For some, this reminds them of their own mortality and may create a fear of death. So if you are younger and your parents or grandparents begin to talk about who died today, be sensitive to them. They may be afraid and not know how to cope with it or express their fears.

Loneliness drives a lot of people to a dark place. Loneliness doesn't discriminate when it comes to our age, gender, culture, or race. Few people enjoy being alone. And those who do enjoy being alone seem to have a choice. But what if you don't have a choice and, for whatever reason, you spend most of your time alone. Are you in a dark place?

If you have found yourself in a dark place, have you been able to get out? If you haven't been able to escape your dark place, why do you think that is? If you have been able to escape your dark place, have you found yourself returning to this dark place more quickly and frequently than you ever thought you would?

If you have found yourself in a dark place, know this: you are not the only one.

More people than you may realize have found themselves in a dark place. Former Olympic gold medalist Michael Phelps continues to speak about his battles with depression or mental health. At the Tokyo 2020 Olympics (held in 2021), Simone Biles withdrew from competition to, in her words, "protect her mental health." Dallas Cowboys' quarterback Dak Prescott revealed he was dealing with depression after the death of his brother and the onset of the coronavirus. WNBA player Liz Cambage and former WNBA All-Star Chamique Holdsclaw have spoken about their depression struggles as well.

I, too, have found myself in a dark place, and I've been there more often than I ever expected. In my journeys to and from my dark place, I've learned and continue to learn some principles, steps, and truths that are helping me to spend more time in the light. I want to share them with you.

This book is about my battles with depression. I'm not excited about being so transparent because some of my experiences are embarrassing. Naturally, they will include my failures and possible triggers, but also my victories. I'm sharing them with you because hopefully they will help you and others reading this book.

Counselors say that there is a depression epidemic among men, especially African American men. Whether you are a man or woman, no matter your culture, you will be exposed here to principles to help you face your fears and alleviate your shame.

I will reveal to you how you can make a non-emotional decision about a tremendously emotional situation. Understanding this one concept will open a door to the light in the midst of your dark place so that you don't have to be imprisoned by your dark place. Isn't this good news?

Unfortunately, I can't guarantee that these practices I'm learning and sharing with you will keep you out of your dark place permanently. For some of you, they might. I believe that, no matter what your situation, some of these steps can improve your situation. But I'm hoping that for all of us, these practices will at the very least lessen our time in our dark places and guide us toward the light.

"This is an exciting truth, that we can play a role in our emotional well-being."

And that these practices will help us to enjoy ourselves and those who love us. This concept is based on Psalm 131:2, which says, "Instead, I have calmed and quieted myself, like a weaned child who no longer cries for its mother's milk. Yes, like a weaned child is my soul within me." This is an exciting truth, that we can play a role in our emotional well-being. This book will be full of suggestions for you to try.

At the end of every chapter are questions to help you process what you have read and your situation. Don't feel pressure to answer any of these questions, and please don't feel overwhelmed by the number of them. Maybe, for you, one question is all you'll be comfortable answering.

Please take this journey with me because I believe it will bring you hope as you see yourself and your situation from a new perspective.

You'll discover that most chapters have three sections. First, I will share my experiences with darkness. Then, to help encourage you, I've asked Dr. Monique Gadson (Dr. Mo) to join me in the discussion from her perspective as a licensed counselor. Dr. Mo helped me escape a very dark place in my life. After I share, Dr. Mo will respond and make suggestions. Then, you have the opportunity to discover more about your own personal journey by working through the mental exercises at the end of each chapter. Neither Dr. Mo nor I want you to be overwhelmed by the end-of-the-chapter exercises, so don't feel that you have to do them all. There is no deadline for completing them. If you have a counselor, you may want him or her to assist you.

But as you engage in these mental exercises, you may discover your triggers and warning signs, place of hurt, healing, hope, and happiness.

Additionally, samples from our text-counseling conversations will be included in the "Dr. Mo's Couch" section throughout the book. In these conversations, I hope that you will see that Dr. Mo has God-given insights and encouragement for me. They show how she gently pressed me at times to examine myself more than I would do by myself. And she kept in contact with me long after I thought I was healed—over the timespan of almost one year. At the writing of this book, she continues to check on me.

To be clear, this book is not attempting to take the place of any professional counselor with whom you may be working. It is a book of hope, written especially for those of you not working with a counselor, that it may provide you with some practical options to experience genuine joy.

I'm so excited that you are reading this book because of the responses I received after teaching about depression at the Fatherhood CoMission and in several churches. The most common responses were, "No one ever talks about depression in church!" and "Your sermon has helped me realize that I'm not crazy!" My prayer is that this book will help you or your family or your friends.

You may be reading this book because you have a loved one who frequents a dark place. This book will help you to better understand and possibly provide love that may be better received after reading it. Some insightful tips for coming alongside a loved one will be given later.

Christina, one of my daughters, gave me permission to share with you a poem she wrote with profound insight into her own personal battle with self and others.

"Shell of an Animal"

Most people see my shell, as I use it to protect me.
I may use my shell to blend in or to be left alone.
Sometimes, I will use it as I reveal hints of myself.
I use my shell to hide my anger, pain, and fear.
In safety, my animal will emerge.

It is my hope that this book will help you emerge in safety. Let's start our new journey toward the light!

WHEN YOU'RE IN A DARK PLACE

CHAPTER ONE

POSSIBLE TRIGGERS FOR OUR DARK PLACE

I was seven years old when I first attended YMCA day camp for seven through eighteen-year-old boys. I was a momma's boy, and this was one of my first times away from her. Mom told me she had arranged for the camp director to have me be his assistant on the opening day. I think she arranged this to make sure that none of the bigger boys bothered me because I was small. It would make me special.

However, the camp director forgot to call me out in front of all the other campers to recognize me as his assistant. I felt so embarrassed and rejected. As soon as Mom picked me up from camp, I told her what didn't happen. She called the director, and he apologized to her. But it didn't make sense to do it after the first day.

Nobody ever seriously bothered me at camp, but the feeling of rejection put a chip on my shoulder that drove me as an athlete to be the best. I was constantly seeking the approval of others for all the wrong reasons. This desire for approval was difficult to satisfy and often led me to a dark place. I learned so many bad lessons that I'm unlearning as an adult.

The feeling of being rejected has been a trigger for me throughout my life. The next chapter will reveal where this and other triggers took me. When thinking about possible triggers that may lead you to a dark place, loneliness (regardless of age), feelings of inadequacy, rejection, or issues related to aging are common for people.

Since many situations can lead us to have feelings of inadequacy and rejection, we'll discuss these issues throughout this book. But I want to give some special attention to loneliness and aging issues as we begin our journey together.

We can find ourselves feeling lonely as a single person, or even if you're in a relationship or marriage, or as we age. All of these concerns can lead us to depression. No matter what the situation, our perspective of ourselves and our situation really can make all the difference as we enter a dark place, affecting whether we stay in a dark place or if we are able to find the light to guide us out of our dark place.

Let's take a brief look at loneliness.

Our society is filled with lonely people. I conduct singles conferences around the country, and "Healing a Broken Heart" is a popular session at these conferences. But "How to Be Single and Content" and "I've Been Lonely Too Long" are easily the two most popular sessions among singles at my conferences.

A few summers ago, a counselor led a workshop for parents of teenagers. He shared that his research and counseling experience revealed that many young people, millennials, and those who are aging are often lonely. What really shocked me is that he mentioned an app that would increase the number of "friends" an individual had on social media. These friends are not real people, only numbers.

Ask yourself: Would it be worse to be popular for a moment and lose it or to never be popular?

What is sad about adding these numbers in order to be popular is that you still don't really have more friends. The people who contact you because of your new popularity will seldom be your friend. They are only associating with you because they believe that association will make them popular. These kinds of people are what my mom called "acquaintances." They won't be there when you want them or need them.

As quickly and frequently as technology changes, there is no telling how social media will be communicating in the future, so all the various social media outlets may cease to be. But what will not cease to be is the human need to be wanted and to be loved!

If you feel that you are not popular and that you are alone, here are a couple of thoughts to consider:

- Proverbs 18:24 says, "A man [or woman] who has friends must himself [or herself] be friendly" (NKJV). A practical application of this verse could be that we need to initiate trying to make a friend by being friendly first to someone else. Maybe you have tried this and it didn't work for you. Be careful as you try to make a new acquaintance that you aren't trying to please that person at all costs. Don't lose who you are in this process. A friend will like you for who you are, including your imperfections. A friend will tell you about your flaws and will try to help you to work on them but will be your friend regardless.

- You need to like yourself. Don't worship yourself, but like yourself. If you don't like you, people can sense this, and it is unattractive—except to those who want to take advantage of you.

- Give away your time to help those who can't repay the favor. This will take your mind off of yourself. And you may receive more than you give.

- Try to reconnect with old friends.

- Spend more time with God.

- Ask and answer the question, "Why, do I hate being alone?"

- Being alone can be a good time to get to know yourself better.

- If you're not content being alone, you won't be content with hundreds of friends.

These tips and more can be found in my singles book, *Single and Free to Be Me.*

Maybe your issue isn't loneliness, but aging. Having played basketball in college and overseas against Olympic and National teams, I find it strange that, sometimes, my body lets me down. I'm over sixty-eight years old, and the sad reality is that I can't do some things that I used to do quite easily.

Several years ago, I tore my meniscus. I couldn't run. I had to be pushed in a wheelchair in order to make my international flight connection in time to conduct a marriage conference with my wife, Brenda, for our military. I felt so bad and useless in that wheelchair. I felt even worse for Brenda. I didn't and don't want her to have to become my caregiver. My situation also played with my idea of manhood. I wrestled with such questions as "Am I really a man anymore?" and "Will Brenda grow to despise me if I'm no longer able to take care of her?"

> "That change in my attitude changed how I felt about myself."

How did I manage this situation? First, I thanked God for the incredible parents he gave me. They both had great genes! How many guys at 5'7" can dunk? Or could dunk? I reviewed my athletic career and had no complaints. I had to embrace my present state. I said to God, "If my body never gets better, I've had a tremendous ride!"

That change in my attitude changed how I felt about myself. Eventually, I had surgery. I'm back to playing tennis, but my body continues to age. I must learn to accept that.

Do I have aging concerns? Sure I do. I definitely don't want to be put in a nursing home. But I may not have a choice. What I can control is deciding not to worry about it now and to face that situation when and if it comes. This kind of mindset gives me peace and keeps my stress low.

We're just getting started here. We're going to address panic attacks and anxiety and so much more. We're also going to show you how God sees you. This may very well blow your mind—in a very good way!

On the next page, you will meet Dr. Monique Gadson, a counselor and PhD who will respond to this chapter. She will give us some amazing insights from her counseling experience and her faith in Christ. We'll call her Dr. Mo because she likes to be informal.

After your time with Dr. Mo, you will have some questions to process. As you start your own journey by answering these questions, you may open doors to experience some emotional freedom.

DR. MO'S COUCH

As Clarence stated, there are numerous factors that can trigger us and send us to this dark place. Sometimes those are obvious. Other times, it might take more introspection to discover what's underneath that trigger.

Loneliness and aging are situations that can propel some into a dark place. Loneliness can result from strained relationships, unhealed wounds, or as a byproduct of some conditions, such as depression. Loneliness can also be a result of losing a loved one or being separated from loved ones geographically.

Aging is a natural event on the spectrum of human development. Typically, we think of older adults struggling with aging, but all adults—young, middle age, and older—can be adversely impacted depending on their life circumstances. There are physical, social, and cognitive considerations in every stage of adulthood. There is something in some area of life that we realize we can no longer do. Young adults realize that, as careers and families take more of their time, some friendships may diminish. Or there may be less time available to devote to some of those relationships. Middle-age adults are dealing with physical changes, older children, and possibly aging parents. Older adults are experiencing loss of loved ones, spouses, or friends. They notice declining health and productivity. For some, it can bring about feeling as if they are in a dark place.

There is so much that can be said about both of these topics. Most individuals will feel lonely at some point in time throughout the course of life. Most will deal with the effects of aging, not only in older adulthood, but quite possibly in the other stages of adulthood. However, I will attempt to brush some broad strokes in order to bring some perspective.

These areas might be associated with an actual or perceived loss of control. At times, when we realize we have no control over some circumstances in our lives, we can possibly find ourselves in a dark place. Because, of course, if we were in control, we would not allow ourselves to experience situations that cause dark places in our lives. The realization of coming to the end of ourselves, and the recognition we are powerless in some events, can lead us to a dark place. Clarence has given some great questions to ponder at the conclusion of this chapter. As we are thinking through our responses, sometimes we find places where we do have some control. It just might not be where we desire.

Another point I'll briefly discuss is that the meaning we associate with loneliness or aging (as well as a host of other thoughts) can give some insight about our being in dark places.

Some people are able to embrace aging with excitement and enthusiasm. They may be looking forward to activities and roles they can enjoy when some of the more major demands of career and family are behind them. Others may dread aging and feel a sense of anxiety. Some may start to feel regretful about things they have not done and think they'll never have an opportunity to do. And again, this can happen in any stage of life. Some young adults may feel they will never marry or have children or leave home if they haven't done so by a certain age. These realizations can send some to a dark place depending on the meaning they associate with their plight. Along with the responses to the questions, I ask you to consider: What does loneliness or aging mean to you? The answers to that question can possibly give significant insights as to why some find themselves in a dark place and some do not.

Consult with a counselor if you find yourself in a dark place for a prolonged time period. Also, consider consulting with a therapist just to dialogue about meanings you associate with these areas.

YOUR JOURNEY

What about you, what has been your experience? Take a few minutes to answer the following questions while considering your life experiences. Name triggers or circumstances that may have caused you to enter into the journey to darkness:

1. _____

_____

2. _____

_____

3. _____

_____

- How do you define loneliness?

- If you are lonely, why do you think you are?

- What could be some benefits of having time to yourself?

- Have you ever thought about helping someone else who could not return the favor when you have been lonely? Will you consider doing that the next time you are lonely? Why or why not?

- What would make you a good friend to have?

- Are you a positive or negative person? Why do you think that is?

- As you age, what are some of the issues with which you struggle?

- How do you feel about yourself as you age?

- What are you grateful for as you age?

- Are you positive or negative in your thoughts about yourself as you age? Why?

CHAPTER TWO

HOW DID I GET HERE?

You'll never be depressed," laughed the late Rushella Latimer when I was younger. She said this because I was always making people laugh! She spiritually mentored me before and after I married Brenda. One of my joys in life was to make Rushella laugh. She had a wonderful and infectious laugh.

I've battled and continue, in some ways, to battle depression. Yet, Rushella's comment is still so clearly etched in my memory. Questions flood my mind: "How did I go from a young man who was never depressed, even during stressful situations, to a man who now periodically wrestles with depression?"

Whether you struggle with rejection, feelings of inadequacy, not being popular, divorce, loneliness, or growing older, if you are ever going to escape your darkness and move toward the light, you must be able to answer the question: *How did I get here?*

> "When I struggled with depression the first time, I didn't realize it until nine months later."

I love to laugh and have fun with people. When I was growing up, my family was poor. No, actually, we were "po." We couldn't even afford the other "or"! Neither could we afford an extra "c" in our last name. So we spent time together telling jokes and trying to make each other laugh. We were poor financially but rich in love and immediate family relationships. Our time together was priceless!

Replaying certain times and situations in my life, I now know that I've been depressed before. When I struggled with depression the first time, I didn't realize it until nine months later.

At that time, the senior pastor of the megachurch on whose staff I served said to me, "I'm not firing you, but I'm eliminating your positions." Seriously, I couldn't understand how the positions of a church's pastor of men's and marriage ministry is eliminated.

What led up to this?

After six months of attending this church, the senior pastor asked me to consider working on staff on a part-time basis. After discussing it with Brenda, my wife, I accepted a position as the marriage ministry pastor. A few months later, I was asked to become the men's ministry pastor too. I also accepted this role. I dramatically reduced my time with the non-profit ministry I had founded, BLR: Building Lasting Relationships, in order to make these ministry positions life-changing ones.

My first year at this megachurch was incredible. Frequently, our chief of staff would come into my office to tell me to go home because I was working too much! She said that she wasn't concerned about my hours but didn't want me to burn out.

Did I mention that I was the first African American to be on staff of this church that, at the time of my joining, was one hundred and thirty-five years old? This church with approximately five thousand members may have had about fifteen African American members, and five of them were my family and me.

This was not the first time that I was the first African American on staff of a predominantly White, Christian, conservative church or non-profit organization.

While the congregation seemed to love having me there, the leadership—specifically, the senior pastor—seemed to struggle with having me on staff. Often he would say to me, "I don't know what to do with you." I was an ordained Baptist minister (this church was a different denomination), a former pastor, the author of several books, the founder and president of a non-profit ministry that had a global reach, a diversity consultant, and a speaker for my ministry and FamilyLife's Weekend to Remember Marriage Getaway Conferences.

After a few more months, this senior pastor began to have me sit in the pulpit and participate in the Sunday church services by either praying or reading Scripture. I wore a suit. The other ministers wore robes. Some members of the congregation complained to him that I should also have a robe. So they ordered a robe with my doctoral insignia. Members of the congregation voiced their appreciation of seeing me in my new robe. This church was very liturgical. Some folks in my culture would call this "High Church." And they would say that I was in "High Cotton"—or, translated, I was doing well.

God was using me in the men's ministry. The three retreats that I organized had a diverse lineup of keynote speakers. Without talking specifically about race, the men of the church loved this cross-cultural experience. At these retreats, several of the men of the church told me they were Democrats but begged me not to tell anyone. Even though politically I'm an independent, I never shared my political affiliation.

At the second retreat, I encouraged the men to bring their sons who were fifteen years of age and older as well as their fathers. I was told by the men that this was the first time the church had three generations of family at a men's retreat: the grandfather, the father, and the grandson. God was moving so powerfully! The men loved this and so did the grandsons! This men's ministry was gaining an identity.

At my last retreat, I challenged the men to show more respect for our senior pastor. It seems that African American and Latino pastors command more respect from the men in their churches than White pastors receive in theirs. I confronted the men that this shouldn't be the case for our senior pastor. I had our senior pastor sit in a chair in the middle of us and had the men lay hands on him and pray for him. Tears rolled down our senior pastor's cheeks.

Unfortunately, after a wonderful time of bonding, our senior pastor left even though he'd previously promised the men that he would stay for the entire men's retreat. The men felt betrayed. They felt that they weren't important enough to him for him to spend time with them. Sadly, it seemed that they were right. The senior pastor left to be in church Sunday morning to appease the biggest tithers in church. What the pastor didn't realize was, if had he been committed to these men, they would have been committed to him financially and taken the pressure of the church budget off of him. He also didn't understand that the senior pastor *is* the men's ministry leader!

But what really was the kiss of death for me was when the senior pastor added me to the preaching rotation. Our church initially had three services when I began preaching, but it quickly moved to five services. I could preach in three, but never all five services. I was the only preacher to be limited to three services. I was the only preacher of color.

After I was given the opportunity to preach, the response from the parents of teenagers was surprising and encouraging. They said, "Our teens don't leave when you are preaching. They feel that you are talking to them. They feel included."

Another factor was that African Americans drove from out of town to hear me preach. Now, more people of color were sitting in the congregation. They were more vocal in their responses to my sermon than the White members of this congregation were.

Then my own flesh unintentionally put the "final nail in my coffin"! After I had preached one Sunday, one of my daughters said, "Daddy, all of your sermon CDs sold out!" The senior pastor's CDs hadn't sold out. As she said this, the senior pastor was standing behind her. He gave me "The Look." The look in his eyes clearly communicated non-verbally that my time on staff was over. I didn't know exactly when, but I knew I was gone.

Eventually, the official day for the official elimination of my positions came.

The senior pastor and the chief of staff held an exit interview with me. They gave me a severance package—two weeks' salary for two years of service to support my wife and three daughters. Shocked by this small severance package, I said, "Normally, a person receives a month's salary per each year of service." The senior pastor angrily responded, "This is a no-fault state, so the church doesn't have to pay you anything! You are lucky to get this pay." My response: "Pastor, you said once that I was funny, but guarded. Your last response was why I was so guarded."

I learned a few years later that the senior pastor gave another former staffer, who was terminated at the same time that I was, a month's severance pay for the year she worked. She was a married, young, White woman with no children, and she received a month's severance pay for the one year she worked. It's tough being an African American male in the Christian conservative community.

No opportunity to say "Good-bye" to the congregation was provided. I left and, unfortunately, left the preaching robe with my doctoral insignia on it.

The church gave me a glowing letter of recommendation. I was told that I wasn't fired, just that my positions had been eliminated.

But I felt fired. And as of today, the church still has these two positions filled. Maybe these two positions were resurrected.

This happened in December right before Christmas. The church leadership told me that it did this to save money on insurance for the upcoming year. Christmas parties were rough that year when people asked what I did and I had to tell them I was unemployed.

Without realizing it, I slipped into depression.

There's a second factor that triggered my depression.

The senior pastor of an African American megachurch in another state asked Brenda and me to become the marriage ministry directors. We had conducted one of our Building Lasting Relationships Marriage Seminars for his church a few years earlier. The pastor discussed salary with us, saying, "There's no one in this church who can do this job." The money he mentioned blew my mind! Even if it had just been me working, we'd be out of debt in three years tops!

Everything was fine until the pastor said, "I want you to go through our marriage committee. Our church is trying to be more corporate." I begged him, "Pastor, please don't do this."

He didn't listen because he thought it was only a formality. The committee behaved irrationally, and its questions were even more bizarre. They promised to get back with me, but they didn't keep their word. Later, I discovered that the committee already had a couple within the church that it wanted for the position, which explained their odd behavior.

The pastor of this megachurch called me and apologized. He said, "The couple that the committee picked can't do what Brenda and you can. I'm going to have to monitor them closely. But if I overrule this committee and bring you two in, it will take three to four years before you can do ministry because there will be resentment." He later gave me a sizeable check. He seemed to feel bad about our experience with his church's marriage committee.

Unknowingly, I felt like a failure.

No income to provide for my wife and children. I kept it all inside and began to rebuild my non-profit that I had put on hold for two years for the sake of working on staff for the predominantly White church.

I was depressed and didn't know it.

When this revelation came to light, I was in Winston-Salem, North Carolina, to officiate the baby dedication for my grand-niece. While there, I spent time with Roger, one of my prayer buddies. I knew him from childhood and old neighborhood. On this same trip, I introduced Roger to David, who at times has been a pastor to me and a prayer warrior for me. It was during my time with Roger and David that I realized I was depressed. They both got me laughing more than I'd laughed in nine months.

Roger had been the ladies' man back in high school. Those girls must have been blind! As Roger shared his story of high school, it filled in the gaps of the last two years of my high school experience at a school I was forced to attend due to integration.

Through Roger's stories, God clearly showed me that he was protecting me even though I didn't know I needed protection and I really didn't want protection in high school.

This knowledge gave me hope, because if God was protecting me then, he certainly was protecting me now! I felt relieved. I immediately felt better physically! I had been carrying much stress and tension for a long time.

These two factors—laughing and seeing God's protection—revealed my depression. I said aloud, "I've been depressed and didn't know it!"

How could I be depressed and not know it? I didn't take time to grieve the loss of and mistreatment from my church position. Neither did I take time to grieve the loss of a promised job in a Black church. I had been looking forward to taking a break from being "the first one" in a White setting as well as having the fellowship of being around Blacks. And I was thinking how I wouldn't have to be bilingual—being Black in a White church.

My second journey into darkness, I was *fully* aware of. It was ten years later when this major depression occurred.

Brenda and I had just returned from conducting our BLR Family Conference in the Grand Cayman Islands. God moved so powerfully as people said their families and marriages were greatly helped. We weren't expecting much in the way of a "Love Offering" for us. But the people surprised us and gave so much more than we could have imagined!

Returning from the islands on cloud nine, I received a voice mail from a multi-billion-dollar company inquiring about my diversity training service.

Did I say multi-billion-dollar company?

Somehow the human resources point person discovered me though my website. He said he loved the video endorsements regarding my biblical diversity seminars as well as my content on my site. This well-known company reaching out to me shocked me. And it gave me hope of a possible big payday!

For the next four weeks, this contact person, along with the vice president of HR, would have two to three phone meetings weekly. This company's president and executive leadership team purchased my diversity book, *Winning the Race to Unity: Is Racial Reconciliation Really Working?* According to the contact person, the executive leadership team loved my book.

The fifth week, they flew me to their headquarters to make a diversity training proposal presentation. My brother-in-law said that companies typically don't pay for a presentation. I had so much help from friends more experienced in working with a secular marketplace. This organization was struggling with its Bible-based principles, yet working in a secular field.

The executive team, which included the president, allotted two hours for my presentation.

My three-hundred-plus ministry prayer warriors were praying for me. Right before the meeting, Stephen Kendrick called to pray with me by phone.

I was feeling good.

From my perspective, the presentation couldn't have gone any better! The president asked me if we could meet a little longer, so the meeting was extended for an additional thirty minutes. He told the vice president of HR to pay me for my presentation. I knew I liked this guy! One vice president asked about my schedule. Dr. Gary Chapman and I were writing the book *Choose Greatness: 11 Wise Decisions That Brave Young Men Make*, but that was it.

After the presentation, the point person said that the president told him, "I really loved Clarence's presentation. Most diversity training is divisive. His presentation brings people together." This point person also said that the president could make this decision on his own.

I never assume that I've landed a contract until one is signed.

But having heard this, having been paid for my proposal presentation, having had Stephen pray for me, having had my three-hundred-plus ministry prayer warriors praying, and having experienced the peace I felt from God regarding my presentation, prematurely I thought I would be hired. Normally, I don't anticipate securing a job. But this one seemed different. It seemed all the signs were saying "Yes!"

Ten days later, I received a call saying that the company was going in another direction. Translation: "We ain't hiring you." Not only was I not hired, but I was not given a reason as to why. This made my situation even worse.

I was devastated! I had let my guard down.

I wondered if their point person set me up. He later revealed to me that he was leaving this company the very next week without telling me why.

Securing this consulting job would have provided life-changing money. This company would have bought my content as well as hired me as the trainer of trainers using my material.

I could have done what they needed in six to nine months.

The rejection blindsided me and just added to my stack of rejections, especially by White conservative evangelicals.

As I told the people who had been praying for me, I didn't want to hear any of the Christian rhetoric such as, "When God closes one door, he opens another" or "Let's praise God anyway." I certainly wasn't feeling that one! Or any of the many other clichés.

I just wanted to be left alone. Again, I felt like a failure and hopeless.

With this life-changing money, I could have taken care of my wife in a way that I have always wanted to for her amazing faithfulness and sacrifices. Her father is a financial success. She's living with a guy who is not. We live by faith via donors and speaking engagements. If you're not the right kind of Black guy, or if you don't have a famous father who is a preacher or speaker, it is difficult, if not impossible, to get on the Christian evangelical conservative speaking circuit.

For about a month, I did little other than feel sorry for myself.

Dr. Monique Gadson is one of my ministry prayer warriors. I shared a little in my ministry newsletter about not getting the consulting job and my negative feelings about it. She read between the lines of my comments in the newsletter. She called and asked if I wanted to talk about it.

I tried to be gracious. But I said, "No thanks."

My initial thought about Dr. Monique's kind offer was that *I* counsel people. I don't need help. I will figure it out.

As soon as I hung up, God said, "You need a counselor." I asked him to counsel me. He repeated, "You need a counselor."

So I called Dr. Monique back and asked her if she would counsel me. She graciously said, "Yes." I told her that I'm not going to use profanity, but I'm pretty raw.

Dr. Monique was and is incredibly amazing! I'll tell you more about her and what she did to help me come out of my dark place in chapter six, "Getting Unstuck."

Another critical piece of my puzzle was my move to a community some called the "Christian Mecca" or "Wheaton West." The majority of this Christian conservative community seemed to be exclusive. If you were different, you might be tolerated, but certainly not celebrated or embraced.

This Caucasian Christian conservative community, I hope unintentionally, consistently labels African American males as the scapegoat for many of the social problems in America. As an African American male, to experience this daily in these Christian workplaces or sometimes even in churches was and is quite depressing.

What about you? What was your experience? Think of your history. Perhaps you were verbally or physically abused, resulting in your experiencing depression. Maybe you don't have many friends and you desperately want to be with people who are not that into you. Or maybe you're aging, and your body or mind isn't cooperating the way you would like. Or maybe, because you are now older, society—including your church—is treating you as though you are invisible.

Or maybe you have not experienced abuse, but you feel that you've consistently been rejected.

It is critical for you, possibly with the help of a counselor, to discover why you may be battling with depression or find yourself in a dark place.

Let's get comfortable as Dr. Mo speaks to us. After our time with her, you can answer some questions that may provide more insight into why we are where we are.

DR. MO'S COUCH

Clarence always gives his all in all to every project. Writing, speaking, counseling—it does not matter the project; he is all in. So what was it about *this* project that caused me to reach out to check on him emotionally and mentally?

As I have already stated, Clarence gives his all with everything. He is just as enthusiastic about something seemingly small as he would be with something seemingly large.

But this project was a bit different.

I think Clarence allowed himself to lean in a bit more and imagine possibilities. It was the feeling of sitting around with friends and family talking about what we would do if we won the lottery. Except no one is close enough to winning a lottery to really depend on that windfall.

Clarence was invited to participate in a project that he could sink his teeth into. This one could be "that one"—that one that could allow him to believe "he has arrived," if you will. The one project that once completed can provide not only physical dividends, but also emotional and mental and even spiritual dividends.

I reached out to him as soon as I read his monthly newsletter.

Clarence is very transparent and forthright about prayer requests on his behalf. After reading about the difficult encounter he experienced, one that was filled with much anticipation, excitement, and promise, I immediately reached out to him. I was privy to some of the things Clarence was working on, so I operated on being a bit more knowledgeable than the general readership.

I asked, "Dude, how are you?" His reply was pretty standard. He was angry. He really did not want to talk about it. Typical.

I said that was fine and I would continue to check in on him. I told him if he wanted to talk, just to reach out and let me know.

Thirty minutes later, I received a text. *Are you free now?*

Yes, I replied.

All I wanted was for Clarence to be okay. But I also knew it would be a process. He did not need to trudge through this experience as much as he needed to sit with it. To realize that God is right there with him. And I knew battle fatigue had begun to set in. He's been going at this a long time now.

It did not matter whether it was clinical, situational, spiritual, or whatever else—I knew it was depression.

I know most men prefer not to speak of the issues and the concerns that plague them. Men are accustomed to "sucking it up," "manning up," and "pushing through" without giving room to create a sacred space—to sit with those emotions that are commonly associated with dark places.

If we are of God, he is always with us. Even in the most devastating of times in our lives, he *is* there. So even as we struggle with the heavy burdens—the mounting loads, the unappreciation, the rejections, the betrayals, the broken promises, the insults, the disparaging stares, and the look-overs—he is there. I imagine us stumbling around in the dark when the power is lost, desperately trying to orient ourselves to the dark. We run our hands ferociously over the walls trying to find a switch to turn on the lights. When we find the switch, we realize it is not that simple. There is more going on than the simple flip of a switch. The power is out. The problem is much larger.

I have come to surmise that if we are indeed Christians, and we follow God, he is always with us (see Matthew 28:20 KJV: "Lo, I am with you alway, even unto the ends of the world"). And I would have to conclude that means also in our dark places. Those dark nights of the soul. The dark months. The dark years. The dark seasons.

Can we think of Daniel in the den of lions?

Can we imagine there is a sacredness in the dark times? If God is there, can we cease striving? Can we sit in the dark for a while with the assurance that God is there also? How might knowing God is there change our experience in the dark place?

Depression is a real situation. A condition. A feeling. However you choose to describe it, it is. There are some who believe it is a disease. Others believe it to be a label. What we can agree on is depression is tough. We can agree that when depression strikes, people will exhibit and experience the "clinical" manifestations of depression.

That is, a loss of interest in things that once brought pleasure. Perhaps a loss of appetite and/or sleep. Or perhaps an increase in eating or sleeping.

WHAT IS DEPRESSION?

I try to assist people and clients with depression by first shifting their thinking and challenging the meaning that is ascribed to depression. Most people do not want to admit they are depressed or might have depression because of the meaning that has been associated with depression.

Depression must be given respect. It has to be given space to explore what it is trying to tell us.

For some, it could mean you are doing too much. You are overwhelmed. You need to rest.

For others, it could mean you have not given enough time to grieving from some sort of loss. That loss could be through death, betrayal, or through natural life rhythms.

We have to learn to become comfortable with that which is uncomfortable.

If we gave depression the sacred space it demands, we could work toward keeping it from consuming us. We would then be in a better position to consume that which depression is trying to offer us. Depression is an opportunity to become intimately acquainted with our mental and emotional status. It is also an opportunity to explore the experiences in life that have eaten away our vigor and vitality and voice, in some instances.

We are ultimately in control of taking the pause. We are in control of what feelings we need to explore. We are in control of the associated works that aid us in facilitating ourselves forward in this process.

Depression can demand or it can invite. I'd rather be invited. If I have to go, I would prefer to be invited and go along rather than for a demand to be placed upon me. I think we feel we have no control. But in reality, we are in control of this process if we submit to depression and what it is inviting us to do, to explore, and even, in some cases, just to be.

If we talk to those who have gone through depression, they can describe that there indeed is joy that is set before you. Especially when we fully embrace and thoroughly process the journey through depression.

I am not saying everyone has to be depressed. I am not saying everyone should wear a sackcloth and sprinkle ashes. But what I am saying is that we should create space for depression. We should create space to acknowledge that one might feel depressed or might be suffering from depression. I think it is not until we normalize that life is *hard* that

Clarence: "God revealed this to me, I wanted respect/revenge and justification from a group of people that don't care about me. But I don't know if I can turn it loose because I wanted it so badly."

Dr. Mo: "Did you come to realize this is a group in general. For example, White people or that specific group for which you did the proposal?"

Clarence: "Certain White Christian evangelicals that I have had and presently interact with. WOW! You made me aware that when I began working for a particular Christian conservative organization that was also political, many of the White men in this organization demeaned Black men directly and me indirectly, making me feel less than equal. So I've been needlessly subconsciously fighting for my respect, equality, defending my race and my manhood. I think God is using you and your questions to free me from my erroneous thinking that I need their approval or even desire it."

Dr. Mo: "Praise God! My next question is what does 'their' respect mean to you?"

Clarence: "I think I was seeking self-validation."

Dr. Mo: "That will help you determine whether you need to still 'fight' for other validations."

Clarence: "I'm done fighting for others' approval."

Dr. Mo: "But you were seeking it for self-approval?"

Clarence: "I wanted equal pay for equal work and the opportunity to advance up the Christian corporate ladder. The environment was constantly demeaning people of color, especially Black males. When you're the first one in the house, it takes a toll on you. On the basketball court, I often won. Even when I didn't, I usually had a fair chance. I could never win with the Christian conservatives, who keep changing the rules. I wanted their respect and financial compensation for my hard work in making this organization better in sensitivity and equality for those who were not White or of their political persuasion."

Dr. Mo: "I'm sure it does. I wonder if you've ever really addressed that feeling? And did this present situation trigger all that wasn't resolved over time? Maybe this is where God is pulling stuff out of you."

Clarence: "No doubt."

Dr. Mo: "This might be the cost of that anointing that will be above what it has been for the work you do now. Pulling down strongholds."

Clarence: "Thanks for challenging me to dig deep today and tonight."

Dr. Mo: "Not that it was my intent, thanks for sharing! I'm sure this is the area being primed by God."

Clarence: "I trust you. I'm processing."

Dr. Mo: "Well, we will see where God is leading and what he's doing."

depression might be understood as a typical response. And some of the experiences and events in and of life are *hard*. And sometimes downright depressing. We have to stop demanding that people must feel happy all the time. We have to stop demanding that people must "get up and get at it."

We have to be okay with people admitting their lived experiences have been difficult and possibly depressing.

To become acquainted with depression, *we* must become familiar. We must know firsthand. We have to allow for the acquaintance with grief. We must fellowship with suffering. Listen to that. It is relationship. We must enter into relationship with depression. And when we learn of depression, when we become familiar with depression, we then one day will experience resurrection power.

But first we must fellowship. Get to know it. What is this all about? What can I do with it? Since I'm here, what can be the benefits of it?

YOUR JOURNEY

A critical key to your healing is knowing how you got here. Remember back to times when you were depressed or in a dark place. List these situations below:

1. _____
   _____

2. _____
   _____

3. _____
   _____

- Based on what you read in this chapter, name the differences between being disappointed and being depressed and what makes them different.

- Are you a female? If "Yes," have you been or are you depressed? Do you ever feel that sometimes, or often, it is gender related? Why? How?

- If you are a person of color, particularly African American, Asian, Latino/Latina, or Native American, do you ever feel that sometimes, or often, your depression is related to your skin color? Why? How?

- If you are an African American male, do you ever feel that you have limited opportunity to get a "fair" chance to advance regardless of your education? Why?

- If you are Caucasian, do you feel that sometimes, or often, you are unfairly made to feel guilty for being who you are? Why do you think this is?

- If you are Caucasian, do you feel that sometimes you are treated as though you don't know what is going on? Do you feel that other cultures condescend to you?

- How and why do you feel your perspective is reality?

- Are you open to having someone close to you evaluate your reality? If not, why not?

- If you're battling with depression, how do you think discussing it in a safe place with a safe person may be helpful?

- Where do you think God is in all of this? Why?

CHAPTER THREE

PANIC ATTACK: WHO WINS?

It was 2 am, and I was wide awake. My mind was racing. What really concerned me was that there was a burning sensation and pain in my left arm. Was this a heart attack? I rubbed my left arm. I took it out from under the covers and rested it on my head. For a while, there was no pain, but my arm got cold because it was January. So I put my arm back under the covers, and the pain quickly returned. Putting it back on my head again didn't alleviate the pain this time.

Now, what do I do? I'd never experienced this burning sensation before.

I needed to calm my heart down. I'd done this before. I took deep breaths. I didn't want a heart attack or stroke. I had just signed up for Medicare and didn't even have my card yet!

I thought my physical issue was all stress related. Mentally, I was overwhelmed! There was so much to do. Yesterday began well, but I didn't put all the time in that I promised myself that I would. I cheated God and myself. I felt guilty and overwhelmed! My bottom line seemed to be that I was not trusting God, so my sleep wasn't sweet as described in Psalm 4:8: "In peace I will lie down and sleep, for you alone, O LORD, will keep me safe." I certainly didn't feel safe with this pain in my arm.

What I really needed to do was pray. So I began talking to God. I asked him to calm my heart. The Holy Spirit reminded me of Philippians 4:13: "For I can do everything through Christ, who gives me strength." This verse became my mantra, as did a couple of other Philippian verses also found in chapter four: "Don't worry about anything; instead, pray about everything. Tell God what you need, and thank him for all he has done. Then you will experience God's peace, which exceeds anything we can understand. His peace will guard your hearts and minds as you live in Christ Jesus" (Philippians 4:6–7). These were inspiring and comforting words. But how did I go from intellectual ascent to believing and experiencing this by faith? I did not demand, but I definitely asked God for his help.

The Holy Spirit reminded me that I was trying to get God on my agenda instead of making sure that I was on his. My agenda was becoming a successful Christian author and speaker, basically making money to support my family and me. But there was also a pride element that drove me to want to feel good about myself.

But I needed to remember that the results were God's, not my responsibility. Thus, the glory was all his, not mine. When I did this, I eliminated the performance aspect of ministry and didn't allow the results to define me. When I worried, like I was doing earlier that morning, I pressed and stressed but definitely did not trust.

I asked God to forgive me for wasting four hours yesterday. I had to trust God for his grace and for him to do whatever he wanted to do with what was before me. I couldn't feel his forgiveness, but I couldn't rely on my emotions then either.

Before I got out of bed, I found myself quoting the Philippians verses again. Somehow, miraculously to me, the pain in my left arm had gone!

I realized that I'd drifted in and out of prayer and sleep. But my prayer had been for others and not myself.

My brief sleep felt good, but I wasn't ready to get up, especially at 4:45 am! I changed my alarm to 4:57 a.m. I got up around 4:52 a.m. because I didn't want the alarm to wake Brenda.

Before I left my bed, I wondered if I would die this morning. There were so many things that I wanted to finish and see before my death. There were at least three or four books that I wanted to have published. At least, I thought, the insurance money would take some financial pressure off of Brenda.

Honestly, thoughts raced through my mind about having a heart attack as I drove to my personal workout trainer Greg's house. What if I crashed Brenda's beautiful new Honda Pilot?

During my fifteen-minute drive to Greg's house, who graciously let me workout with him for free (my favorite price), I listened to gospel music. I clicked on the Donnie McClurkin station on my Apple Music. I listened to gospel music styles that I normally wouldn't. But the lyrics were so powerful and timely to my situation that I couldn't turn it off. This station played all kinds of worship music. As I listened to this worship music, it was transforming my mindset. It reminded me of Romans 12:2: "Don't copy the behavior and customs of this world,

"This transformation was moving me from intellectual knowledge to heart experience."

but let God transform you into a new person by changing the way you think. Then you will learn to know God's will for you, which is good and pleasing and perfect."

Quoting the Philippians verses and listening to worship music based on God's word were transforming my mind and subconsciously changing my emotional state. This transformation was moving me from intellectual knowledge to heart experience. The truths of God's word were changing my thinking and my emotions. This resulted in me beginning to experience peace, hope, and less stress.

After I arrived at Greg's house, he and his friend Matt began to physically work on my body, and that exposed areas of weakness and poor balance. This wasn't a fun thing to do. But at my age, I have to keep moving so I can keep moving. The physical exercise increased my blood-flow circulation, and the endorphins made me feel better. Of course, I really felt good *after* the workout was over. Fortunately, the time usually went by quickly!

As I drove home after this workout, I felt so much better physically, emotionally, and spiritually. No longer was there any pain in my left arm. No longer did I feel overwhelmed. I felt peace. God reminded me that he's in charge and that he can do the impossible. So it doesn't matter how much I've messed up or feel I'm behind. God is the game changer!

I continued listening to the Donnie McClurkin station as I drove home. This gospel music was renewing my mind and emotions.

Suddenly, I realized I had just experienced a panic attack!

This panic attack was a battle for my mind. And if it was a battle for my mind, then who was fighting for control of my mind? It could have been Satan and God, it could have been Satan and me, and it could have been God and me. God won this battle for me.

Initially, I was losing this battle for my mind.

If you have panic attacks, who usually wins? Do you need a new winner? If so, what are you going to do about it?

What caused my panic attack? I have to admit to myself that I'm the reason for my panic attack. My insecurity, my laziness, my dealing poorly with rejection, my fear of rejection, my attachment of failure to rejection (often my rejection is accompanied with my perception of injustice), and my definition of success caused my panic attack.

Intellectually, I know that I'm God's servant and that all I do should be about him and his glory, not mine.

Yet I often battle with my thoughts of being well paid, well thought of, and in high demand.

God has very clearly said, "If I make you famous, it won't be done by man. And if I make you famous, can you handle the constant demand for you?" Then, he asked me, "Why do you want the approval of people who don't care about you? Why don't you let me match you with people who want the gifts I've given you?"

This is the primary battle that goes on in my mind.

In the next chapter, we'll see that there is a difference between a panic attack and anxiety.

Let's see what Dr. Mo has to say. Then, let's answer some questions that will help us better evaluate ourselves and our situation.

DR. MO'S COUCH

At first glance, it really does seem that Clarence might have experienced a panic attack. Most people may associate panic attacks with anxiety or anxiety disorders. However, panic attacks can occur in the context of depressive disorders. According to the Diagnostic and Statistical Manual of Mental Disorders (DSM-V), panic attacks are defined as the following:

> An abrupt surge of intense fear or intense discomfort that reaches a peak within minutes, and during which time four (or more) of the following symptoms occur:

- Palpitations, pounding heart, or accelerated heart rate.

- Sweating.

- Trembling or shaking.

- Sensations of shortness of breath or smothering.

- Feelings of choking.

- Chest pain or discomfort.

- Nausea or abdominal distress.

- Feeling dizzy, unsteady, light-headed, or faint.

- Chills or heat sensations.

- Paresthesias (numbness or tingling sensations).

- Derealization (feelings of unreality) or depersonal-
  ization (being detached from oneself).

- Fear of losing control or "going crazy."

- Fear of dying.

Unless you have previously been diagnosed with panic attacks, please consult with your medical doctor to rule out more serious conditions. Even if you have recently seen your doctor, but never discussed what you may think might be a panic attack, I urge you to make an appointment with your doctor to inform him or her of this newfound experience.

When we are emotionally and mentally overwhelmed, a panic attack might result. After a doctor assesses there is no serious condition that could be underlying, it is prudent that you stop and determine why your body is responding with a panic attack. Could your body be signaling that something else needs to be addressed? Something spiritual? Mental? Emotional?

Clarence took a mental inventory of what was happening within him and around him. He acknowledged the deadlines, other pressures, and his feelings of being overwhelmed.

If you're unable to land on exactly what that "something else" could possibly be, I suggest that you consider speaking with a professional counselor. Some people have much trepidation about sitting with and thinking of what the triggers are. They may get close to naming them and back away. Or they may avoid it altogether. These responses might be best approached with a professional therapist who assists with discovering and identifying those triggers. The therapist will work to ensure that you are equipped with adequate coping resources as you begin the process of dealing with triggers. Listening to music, exercising, praying, and meditating are some options that can be employed to help us manage feelings of stress and being overwhelmed.

By the very nature of a panic attack, it can come "out of the blue." Sometimes, there is no identifiable trigger. You do feel out of control and as though you are losing your mind, as previously stated. And because at times you cannot prepare for these unexpected attacks, it is possible to feel as though you never have control. You might feel as though you're drowning or being consumed.

How then do we cope? When it does not seem that we can answer the questions about panic attacks, what do we do? What if they don't go away? Again, I urge you to seek out a psychiatrist, psychologist, or professional counselor to discuss various remedies and coping resources.

And, as Clarence did, you can always pray. He prayed. He also saturated his mind with a few memorized verses and with the word of God through music. In his experience, the verses and Christian music transformed the way he was thinking, which positively impacted his emotions and actions. Be mindful of God's word recorded in Isaiah 43:2: "I will be with you when you pass through the waters, and when you pass through the rivers, they will *not* overwhelm you. You will not be scorched when you walk through the fire, and the flame will *not* burn you" (HCSB, emphasis mine).

YOUR JOURNEY

I shared my experience with a panic attack. What about you? Do you have an ongoing battle for your mind? Let's look at what your issues are and who the key players are.

If or when you experience a panic attack, name three things that you can identify as possible triggers:

1. _____

   _____

2. _____

   _____

3. _____

   _____

- Why are these issues triggers for you?

- When you are in the midst of your panic attack, how do you feel about yourself and why?

- Do you feel you are out of control of yourself or mind during your panic attack? If yes, why?

- Do your feelings lead you to take certain actions? If so, name them.

- Why do you think your feelings lead you to take these actions?

- Consider honestly: Are these actions productive or self-destructive?

- If your actions are productive, what do you do, and why are these actions productive for you?

- Do these productive actions help bring you out of your depression or panic attack?

- If your actions are self-destructive, what do you do? Why are these actions destructive for you, even if you don't think they are obvious to others?

- Can you name what causes your panic attack to end?

- After your panic attack, do you feel that you are back in control of yourself? Why or why not?

- After your panic attack, how do you feel about yourself? Why?

- If you can tell when you are in a panic attack, that is a form of awareness. When you are aware that you are in a panic attack, do you think you could attempt to apply principles to help you shorten or terminate the attack?

- Are you willing to face the things that are triggers for you?

CHAPTER FOUR

FACING ANXIETY

Anxiety is common and maybe even natural for most people. It is common for most men, regardless of age, to be nervous or feel some anxiety when attempting to tell a woman that they like them. Some females experience anxiety when hoping a certain someone will notice them. Some of us may experience anxiety when trying out for a team, applying to college, or interviewing for a job. Some of us may have anxiety when and if we have to speak in public.

These experiences I would label as short-term natural anxiety.

My anxiety, I believe, goes beyond what is normal. But Dr. Mo will let us know more at the end of this chapter.

From my limited perspective, there is a difference between experiencing anxiety and a panic attack. For me, a panic attack is sudden or out of the blue. Typically, I don't have time to prepare for it because it is unexpected.

When I experience anxiety, usually it is connected to an upcoming event. Often, I begin to get nervous because I dread it, fearing that I won't do well or that it will be an unpleasant situation.

PERFORMANCE ANXIETY

One key area of anxiety for me is playing competitive tennis. I may give you more information than you want to know, but I believe it lays a crucial foundation for you to understand my battle with anxiety.

From the mid-'80s until about twelve years ago, I was an extremely good tennis player and often won singles tournament championships.

In my thirties, former basketball coaches and peers said that I was an exceptionally good athlete, having competed well in basketball internationally, including against Olympic players. One of my former college basketball coaches said that he could arrange a tryout for me for one NBA team because he knew the general manager.

After graduating from Southwestern Baptist Theological Seminary in 1983, I moved to Tulsa, Oklahoma, for a ministry opportunity.

There, I met Rudy in a tennis store. He became one of my best friends. We were both single and loved playing tennis. Rudy played tennis at the University of Southern California. He was a big-time player and tall at 6'2".

BECOMING A TENNIS CHAMPION

Rudy graciously worked on my game. He was the tennis pro for a country club, and he let me hit with him for free at least three times weekly. He introduced me to other tennis teaching pros and players.

Eventually, I was playing tennis three to four hours daily.

Rudy got me into playing tournaments. He had me start at the lowest level at the time, 3.0. I won the Tulsa City championship at that level. I was nervous about playing in a championship, but then, I said to myself, "I don't know if I'll get back here, so I might as well win it today." My preparation with Rudy made it an easy win.

Then, I moved up to the next level of competition, 3.5, and won another tournament. I moved up to 4.0 and won another championship.

My next challenge was to begin playing at the next level that was called "Open." These were tournaments in which college players and anyone who thought they were good enough competed for cash instead of a trophy!

Through the years, marriage, family, and work significantly limited my tennis time.

My last championship was in a 4.0 league at my old club in 1997 in Colorado Springs, Colorado.

THE PRESSURE OF EXPECTATIONS

I loved being asked to play Number One singles for local United States Tennis Association (USTA) tennis teams. I expected to win and was expected to win by my teammates. The team that won the city league advanced to the district championship. If a team won the district championship, it went to the sectional, and then to the national.

Why am I telling you all this? What I've described to you is foundational for the pressure I faced! Everyone was there to win and advance.

My first year playing USTA team tennis in Colorado Springs, my team won the Colorado Springs league and advanced to the districts in Denver, Colorado.

As teams were put together, it was very competitive. Some teams got illegal players, who should have played at least one level up in competition but somehow get into lower leagues.

Unfortunately, during the matches, there was no official to call whether the ball is in or out, resulting in some questionable calls. Usually, you played before a crowd, so there was additional pressure to win.

Hall of Fame tennis great Billie Jean King says, "Pressure is a privilege." Some of the Chicago young men I coached in basketball in the 1970s often said, "Pressure cooks a goose." Translation: some people crack under pressure.

MY PAIN: GOING FROM A WINNER TO A LOSER

Approximately, twelve years ago, I was playing Number One singles for a USTA team. While practicing on my serve, I felt a sharp pain run through my spine. It hurt and scared me! Immediately, I changed my service motion during the middle of this season. That was a major mistake.

I lost confidence in my serve, and the rest of my game deteriorated. With no confidence and mental toughness, it is difficult to do a lot of things well. I don't think I won another match that season. Everyone saw me lose a lot of matches. I was so embarrassed by my consistent losing, and I didn't think well of myself.

For the first time in decades, I remembered what it was like to lose and not have confidence under pressure. I hadn't felt this way since junior high.

The next season, there were no calls from any team for me to play singles. My USTA days seemed to be over due to my choking in singles and doubles. I hate to admit it, but I was okay with this. I was tired of losing to players I should beat. I was tired of the pressure.

I was losing because of my fear of losing and the pressure I felt from others and myself to win. It is one thing to go from a loser to a champion, which I had done back in my transition from junior high to winning in high school and college in basketball. But reverting back to a loser after having been a champion was so much more painful! And the competition in

Colorado Springs wasn't close to the competition I had in Tulsa. I thought, "This is what it feels like to be average and to lose." It was so devastating because so much of my identity was tied to my winning. This had been my way of proving my manhood and that I belonged.

BABY STEPS TO LEARNING HOW TO WIN AGAIN

Approximately, four years ago, I connected with a local successful high school coach, Dave Lehman, who was also the teaching pro at my former club. I took some tennis lessons from him and saw some major and quick improvements in my game. He was so encouraging. To my surprise, he asked if I would just like to hit with him for free! Hitting with Dave is like getting a free tennis lesson! I was all over this.

I thought that, with his help, I would begin playing USTA tennis tournaments again, maybe in two years. I thought that no one would ever ask me to play on a USTA team again.

But to my surprise, Scott, a friend from my old club's Friday morning league, asked me to play doubles with him. I asked Scott to have his sons read my then-book project, *Choose Greatness: 11 Wise Decisions That Brave Young Men Make*. It made us closer.

I was hoping to spend this year improving my game and then, hopefully, play USTA the next year. Suddenly, next year was now. I agreed to play with Scott because it was an honor to be asked by him. Scott is one of the best singles players in town, so for him to play with me, he was sacrificing his singles game—just for me.

I was so nervous about playing doubles because I didn't want to let my tennis partner and USTA team down.

Our first match couldn't have gone any better! My first shot I hit off my tennis racquet frame for a winner. Scott encouraged me. His encouragement off such a lucky shot was all I needed!

I played the best I've played in competition in years! Other members of our team were watching and asked if I was old enough to play on another team. Often players play on more than one team in different age groups or ranking divisions. What a tremendous compliment after years of losing and feeling so inferior!

But in our next home match, I was defeated by my anxiety. It was a close match, but we lost because of my fear of missing my return of my opponents' serve. When you think about missing, you tend to become a self-fulfilling prophecy. I was so worried about missing that I wasn't focusing on the ball, I was looking at my opponent serving and the crowd that included my teammates.

After we lost 6–4, 6–4, I told Scott that I had choked and said that I was sorry. He looked shocked. I'm not sure he has heard many guys admit to choking.

Our next match changed my approach to anxiety forever.

The following week, our opponents weren't as good as the ones we had lost to the previous week. Yet we lost the first set quickly, only winning one or two games. We were the last match of the night. After we lost the first set so badly, the rest of our team went home except our captain, who had to stay in order to record our score, and Jeff, a teammate with whom I had done relationship counseling.

As we started the second set, I began to pray, "God, help me see the ball." I did not ask God to let us win because I didn't think that was a fair prayer.

I did pray, asking God to help me see the ball. I began to silently recite Philippians 4:13: "For I can do everything through Christ, who gives me strength." It became my mantra. I began to focus on the ball. Then, I began to return my opponents' serve consistently. This second set was close. But we never led until we got into a seven-point tiebreaker (first team to seven points and a two-point difference wins) to win the second set. We got ahead in the tiebreaker, and I said to Scott, "We can win this thing!" He got confident! We both played so much better. We won the second set with the crowd watching! My left-handed serve became a huge factor. Then, we won the third set, a ten-point tiebreaker (the first team to ten points with a two-point margin wins). We won 1–6, 7–6, 10–7, and people went crazy!

"Notice as I faced my anxiety, it was not with extreme confidence. I faced my fear, I focused, I asked for help, and my emotions changed from thinking the worse to thinking I could do better."

For me, I won twice! I faced my anxiety and defeated it! As my emotion changed, that influenced my confidence, which impacted my physical play.

People said I was the hero! It had been a long time since I'd heard that! I savored that win. Even the following week, people were still talking about that match!

ADMIT HOW YOU ARE FEELING

I wish I could tell you that anxiety is never an issue for me anymore, but I'd be lying.

You can face your anxiety too. Notice that, as I faced my anxiety, it was not with extreme confidence. I faced my fear, I focused, I asked for help, and my emotions changed from thinking the worse to thinking I could do better. My hope translated into positive physical action. Then, with simply hitting the ball back, my confidence grew.

You can do the same with whatever you are facing, whether it is the fear of possible rejection, fear of being alone, or fear of having memory or physical issues due to aging.

Facing my anxiety is not as traumatic as it used to be. This emotional victory experienced in my doubles match has become a foundation for facing any new anxious situation. It has become a mental trophy to which I often refer while playing tennis. It's not in the winning, but it is all in what I'm focusing on. It is easy to be distracted by the crowd, my teammates, and my opponents. But what I need to focus on is the ball that is on my side of the net that is within my hitting zone.

As previously mentioned, I still struggle with anxiety. But I have learned some takeaways from my battle in facing it that I'd like to share.

- I don't have to continue to be defeated by my anxiety. This is tremendous news for me. I hope it is for you too!

- Admit to yourself that you are feeling anxiety or fear toward a particular situation. Not admitting that you have anxiety may result in no change to your emotional status or a worsening of it. No change in our emotions causes us to be *stuck* emotionally.

- If you're playing a sport, anxiety can make your muscles tight instead of being loose.

- After admitting to yourself that you have anxiety, you must figure out a way to face your anxiety.

- Simply embracing the idea of facing your anxiety can be a source of hope for you. Hope for change may create a new beginning for you or a foundation for change for you. It may become a positive distraction from your anxiety.

- Develop a plan to face your anxiety. Maybe the first step in your plan is to simply admit it to yourself when you feel anxiety.

- Asking for help during your anxiety is not a sign of weakness. It is actually a sign of strength.

- It seems the best way to face your anxiety is during the time you are most fearful or stressful.

- Often, I believe that what we're facing is not as great as our mind makes it.

- Learn to give yourself grace; the way God gives us grace. In a recent USTA tennis season, which I had not planned to play, I played a doubles match. Quickly, I discovered that I had the wrong eye contacts in, so the ball was blurred to me. My partner was facing his archrival. He seemed to mentally check out. We got killed and lost this match. I have a peace about it because of the circumstances. I gave myself grace and didn't feel bad about it. Nor did I beat myself up. In fact, it inspired me to practice to get better—and to make sure I have the correct contacts in before the match.

- I believe it is okay to get anxiety, but you don't have to stay in a fearful or stressful state. That is not healthy or helpful for you.

- Possibly, a beneficial and practical method to alleviate your anxiety is to prepare for it. The more I practice for my matches, the less anxiety I experience. The more I practice speaking for an event, the less nervous I am when it is time to speak. Each time a match begins, I'm nervous, which is normal. But as I focus on hitting the ball, good things happen.

- Another tennis pro, Dave Scott, has really simplified my game so there is less clutter in my head.

- During one of our practice sessions, Dave put a tarp over the net so I couldn't see where my ball landed on his side of the net. He said, "What happens on the other side of the court is none of your business. You need to focus on your side of the net or focus only on what you can control." So I'm concerned about other circumstances, but I focus only on what I can control. Then, I remember Philippians 4:13: "For I can do everything through Christ, who gives me strength."

Anxiety, like a panic attack, doesn't have to control you or ruin your life. There is hope for you. You may be able to help yourself by using some of the principles in this book or possibly engage the help of a professional counselor like Dr. Mo.

Nothing is necessarily wrong with us if we experience anxiety. But we may be able to lessen the effect of anxiety in our lives.

Let's see what Dr. Mo has to say. Then, let's answer some questions that will help us better evaluate ourselves and our situation.

DR. MO'S COUCH

Anxiety is quite a complex topic. There are many types of anxiety disorders such as social anxiety disorder, generalized anxiety disorder, and agoraphobia. It seems what Clarence experienced is performance anxiety.

Because anxiety can be a symptom and a state, it is difficult to encompass everything that can be discussed about anxiety. What I will talk about is when you should seek professional help. If Clarence had persisted in avoiding playing tennis again, I would have advised him to speak with a counselor. We do not want anxious tendencies to progress to avoidant behaviors.

Since there are many categories of anxiety disorders, I will discuss Generalized Anxiety Disorder. According to *The Diagnostic and Statistical Manual of Mental Disorders, 5th Edition,* there are several factors that distinguish generalized anxiety disorder from nonpathological anxiety:

- The anxiety is excessive and interferes with everyday functioning.

- The anxiety is more pervasive and distressing.

- Physical symptoms are present such as restlessness, feeling keyed up, difficulty concentrating, and muscle tension, just to name a few.

When anxiety is excessive and has lasted for more than six months, if it is not due to substance use or side effects of medication or a medical condition, or not explained as part of another mental disorder, you should seek out

Dr. Mo: "How are you?"

Clarence: "I'm good thanks to God using you and others to help me. God had me do a devotional at the Fatherhood Summit. The response blew me away! People went crazy saying how it helped them. People took pictures of all my PowerPoint slides! I made it into a sermon, and I preached it last Saturday and Sunday. It is entitled, 'Biblical Tips for When You're in a Dark Place.' "

Dr. Mo: "Ammmmmmmeeennnnnn!!! All for his glory! I came to realize that warfare comes against me when I start to write. I thought about how you would pray for protection as you write..."

Clarence: "I shared Philippians 3:12–21 NLT, 'I don't mean to say that I have already achieved these things or that I have already reached perfection. But I press on to possess that perfection for which Christ Jesus first possessed me. No, dear brothers and sisters, I have not achieved it, but I focus on this one thing: Forgetting the past and looking forward to what lies ahead, I press on to reach the end of the race and receive the heavenly prize for which God, through Christ Jesus, is calling us. Let all who are spiritually mature agree on these things. If you disagree on some point, I believe God will make it plain to you. But we must hold on to the progress we have already made. Dear brothers and sisters, pattern your lives after mine, and learn from those who follow our example. For I have told you often before, and I say it again with tears in my eyes, that there are many whose conduct shows they are really enemies of the cross of Christ. They are headed for destruction. Their god is their appetite, they brag about shameful things, and they think only about this life here on earth. But we are citizens of heaven, where the Lord Jesus Christ lives. And we are eagerly waiting for him to return as our Savior. He will take our weak mortal bodies and change them into glorious bodies like his own, using the same power with which he will bring everything under his control.'"

professional help. Anxiety that needs to be addressed by a mental health clinician causes significant disruption in day-to-day living. Also, if you find that it is difficult to control the anxiety, you really should seek counseling. The counselor will evaluate and determine if a referral is needed to a medical doctor or psychiatrist for medication to be prescribed.

YOUR JOURNEY

Like tennis pro Dave Scott said, "What happens on the other side of the court is none of your business. You need to focus on your side of the net or focus only on what you can control." Let's dig into what you have control over.

Do you feel that your anxiety is usually connected to a scheduled event, short or long-term, that you dread?

Name an event or events in your life that create anxiety for you.

1. _____

_____

2. _____

_____

3. _____

_____

- Why do these events cause anxiety for you?

- What do you do when you are in the midst of your anxiety?

- Do you feel defeated by your anxiety?

- What causes your anxiety to fade or cease? Does it disappear because the event is over?

- What in this chapter encourages you to face your anxiety?

- Is this encouragement significant to you? If so, why is it significant?

- Does your faith, reading the Bible, or praying play a role in your battle with anxiety? How?

FINDING
HOPE

CHAPTER
FIVE CHA
IVE CHAPTER
FIVE

THE BATTLE FOR YOUR MIND

*But there is another power within me that is at war
with my mind.* —Romans 7:23 NLT

*For as he [or she] thinks within himself [or herself],
so he [or she] is.* —Proverbs 23:7a NASB

I'll never forget the first time I played basketball in a new city at
a downtown megachurch's gym. Businessmen, former college
players, and a current European professional played there. In my
first game, under the basket, a 6'8" player hit me with his hips
and sent me flying and sliding about fifteen feet. My sweaty body
aided my sliding.

All the other players laughed. I didn't think it was funny. I
was the only Black person in the gym, so I don't know if this was
racial or not. But I was furious!

As a Black man in America, my initial thought regarding how
this situation made me feel was "Here we go again!" Why didn't
at least one of the White players say this was wrong—no justice?
"That's okay," I said to myself. I created my own justice. Yes, I
had issues!

The 6'8" player was a good one, but he had a bad habit of bringing the ball down to his waist after a rebound. This placed the ball within my reach. Instead of trying to take the ball, I would hit his arms as hard as I could, then say, "My foul, your ball." I was ready for a fight, but this tall guy never said a word or even gave me a nasty glare.

When I was on offense and driving to the basket, I said derogatory things about him and his mother as I scored.

After the time for playing basketball ended, we all had to shower and return to work. The Holy Spirit convicted me of my sin. I found this guy in the locker room and apologized. He was shocked! He simply said, "It is just basketball."

This guy wasn't a racist. He was just immature in some of his actions on the basketball court—just like I was.

THE FIGHT OF TWO WOLVES WITHIN YOU

When you're in a dark place, or at least when I'm in a dark place, what I'm thinking in that moment is critical as to how I feel about myself and, ultimately, what actions I take as a result of my thoughts.

Sometimes, I need to evaluate the source of what I'm mentally trying to process and why I'm thinking a particular way. As a Christ follower, I have to discern who is talking to me. Is it God communicating with my own thoughts, another power, or a negative one (Satan making suggestions to me)?

Often, it seems like I'm hearing three different voices. But two of them can be similar. God is telling me one thing, and Satan is telling me to do the opposite of whatever God is saying. My voice may be similar to Satan's voice, especially if I'm having a pity party.

If you are not familiar with the Bible, the first book, Genesis, tells the story of Eve, the first woman created by God.

Eve wrestled with her understanding that she and Adam, her husband, were not to eat the fruit of the tree in the middle of the garden of Eden. But Satan, God's enemy, constantly urged her to eat from this tree because Satan implied that God was holding out on her. Satan told Eve that if she ate the fruit of this particular tree, she would become just like God. This was something God had already given Eve. While being tempted by Satan, she only heard that there could be something more. She already possessed what Satan was promising to give her.

It seems that the last voice that we listen to is the one that we often follow.

As I was discussing the writing of this chapter with Steve, my chiropractor, he suggested this Cherokee legend about an old Cherokee grandfather teaching his grandson about life:

> "A fight is going on inside me," he said to the boy. "It is a terrible fight and it is between two wolves. One is evil—he is anger, envy, sorrow, regret, greed, arrogance, self-pity, guilt, resentment, inferiority, lies, false pride, superiority, and ego."
>
> He continued, "The other is good—he is joy, peace, love, hope, serenity, humility, kindness, benevolence, empathy, generosity, truth, compassion, and faith. The same fight is going on inside you—and inside every other person, too."
>
> The grandson thought about it for a minute and then asked his grandfather: "Which wolf will win?"
>
> The old Cherokee simply replied, "The one you feed."[1]

So how do we decide which voice that we should follow? Consider asking yourself a series of questions. These questions may help you make a wise decision as to which voice you should follow:

- What are the short-term and long-term consequences regarding each voice to which I am listening?

- Are these thoughts positive and productive or are these thoughts negative, self-degrading, hurtful to others and/or myself, and ultimately destructive?

- Are these thoughts encouraging me to be selfish?

- Are these thoughts encouraging me to consider God's options for me?

- Will this have a negative or positive effect on my health?

- How will this impact my ability to think clearly?

- How will this decision impact my family or others who care about me?

- Is this decision morally right or wrong?

- Am I being influenced by others to do something I really don't want to do?

- Will I stand up for what I know is right rather than give in to the pressure of others?

- Is this decision consistent with what I believe about God?

- Will I be glad that I made this decision five years from now?

- Does this decision help me become the person I want to be?[2]

When trying to distinguish between God's voice and Satan's voice, an understanding of what they emphasize will help.

God emphasizes the eternal. In 2 Corinthians 4:18, it says, "So we don't look at the troubles we can see now; rather we fix our gaze on things that cannot be seen. For the things we see now will soon be gone, but the things we cannot see will last forever." Hebrews 11:1 states, "Faith is the confidence that what we hope for will actually happen; it gives us assurance about the things we cannot see."

Satan emphasizes the temporal.

God focuses on long-term consequences.

Satan stresses immediate gratification.

God emphasizes the lasting effect.

Satan maximizes momentary feelings.

God emphasizes "seeing the big picture."

Satan amplifies "having fun now!"

Satan will even tell us that God will forgive us for any pleasurable act of disobedience to God we commit. It is true that God will forgive us for our disobedience. But what Satan conveniently doesn't tell us is that there are certain consequences for our actions that disobey God. Satan is good at mixing God's truth with his lies.

God certainly forgives our sin. Psalm 103:12 reads, "He [God] has removed our sins as far from us as the east is from the west." And in 1 John 1:9, it is stated, "But if we confess our sins to him, he is faithful and just to forgive us our sins and to cleanse us from all wickedness."

When Satan encouraged Eve to eat of the forbidden fruit from the tree in the garden of Eden in Genesis 3, he didn't tell Eve of the consequences of her disobedience. Here are two consequences according to Genesis 3:16: "I will sharpen the pain of your pregnancy, and in pain when you give birth. And you will desire to control your husband, but he will rule over you."

These weren't all the consequences for Eve, her husband, or for Satan.

One has to wonder whether, if Eve had known of these consequences ahead of time, would she have still disobeyed God?

The Bible is full of individuals who listened to Satan, disobeyed God, asked God for forgiveness, received it, and then still experienced some of the consequences of their sin.

THE PROGRESSION OF SIN IN THE MIND

This progression of sin in our minds is found in James 1:13–15: "And remember, when you are being tempted, do not say, 'God is tempting me.' God is never tempted to do wrong, and he never tempts anyone else. Temptation comes from our own desires, which entice us and drag us away. These desires give birth to sinful actions. And when sin is allowed to grow, it gives birth to death."

These verses outline the progression of sin. First, we have an evil thought. This thought may come from Satan or us. Once we decide that we are going to do the wrong thing, we rationalize it to ourselves, thus justifying our wrong thought. Next, we compromise our standards or morals. At this point, it is difficult to stop our momentum of disobedience, resulting in losing control and participating in an action that we ourselves would normally disapprove of, as does God.

Unfortunately, in my late twenties, while single, I became addicted to pornography. After getting married, I assumed my addiction would end. It did not. After eleven years of addiction, God delivered me from my pornography obsession.

When I was caught up in my pornography addiction, I was a Christian. But I lived a double life. When tempted to view pornography, seldom did I resist this temptation. So I rationalized and justified it. Then, I would watch it. Next, I immediately felt guilty. I was a slave to my addiction. Finally, it was this realization of my slavery to pornography that was my first step to breaking my addiction. I had to admit to myself that I was addicted to pornography and that I needed help. I definitely asked God to help, and he did.

THERE'S A BATTLE FOR YOUR MIND

Whether it is feelings of rejection, inadequacy, loneliness, lack of popularity, or age-related issues that have driven you to a dark place, it is really a battle for your mind. Indeed, there is a battle between God and Satan for your mind.

Our minds have power. Proverbs 23:7a reads, "For as he [or she] thinks within himself [or herself], so he [or she] is" (NASB). We need to be aware of this power and use it appropriately.

Our internal thinking influences who we are and what we do. We seem to have a choice according to Proverbs 16:32, which says, "Better to be patient than powerful; better to have self-control than to conquer a city." Self-control is one of the fruits of the Holy Spirit given to Christ followers. It is mentioned in Galatians 5:22–23. So we do have a choice in regard to controlling ourselves. This is good news! We are not enslaved, and we don't have to be!

"Our internal thinking influences who we are and what we do."

Even if Satan or we give ourselves an evil thought, we can ask God to take away such a thought that is not of him according to 2 Corinthians 10:5b: "And we are taking every thought captive to the obedience of Christ" (NASB). When I have a thought that is evil or a temptation, my prayer is this: "Lord, I don't want to think about these thoughts. Please take them away from me." It's that simple!

First John 5:14–15 states, "And we are confident that he hears us whenever we ask for anything that pleases him. And since we know he hears us when we make our requests, we also know that he will give us what we ask for." Therefore, based on what these two verses say, we know that if we pray according to his will, God will say "Yes" to our prayer.

God says in Jeremiah 29:11, "'For I know the plans I have for you,' says the LORD. 'They are plans for good and not for disaster, to give you a future and a hope.'" So God himself doesn't want us to be in a bad place or a dark place. He wants us to be in a good place.

One of the key skirmishes in the battle for our mind is the reality that there are some memories that have scarred us so badly that we simply can't forget them. The Bible doesn't teach forgetting, so our ability to forget or not forget is not a faith issue.

WHAT IS IMPOSSIBLE TO FORGET?

Remember the 6'8" player I mentioned earlier? He became a good friend. We even played in a league together. A few years later, he died. I'm so glad we became friends so my memories of him were good. Did I ever forget our first encounter? No. How did I deal with it? I remembered it every time I saw him. But I said to myself, "No big deal, we're friends."

It's impossible to forget and let go of a grudge or resentment without forgiving.

The goal of forgiveness is not forgetting, even though that sometimes happens. The goal of forgiveness is treating that person as though it never happened. Forgiveness does not eliminate accountability, restitution when needed, or responsibility.

Forgiveness is more of an action than an emotion. This is why God can command us to love our enemies like he does in Matthew 5:44–46: "But I say, love your enemies! Pray for those who persecute you! In that way, you will be acting as true children of your Father in heaven. For he gives his sunlight to both the evil and the good, and he sends rain on the just and the unjust alike. If you only love those who love you, what reward is there for that?"

It seems that God's love is an action. As we do the right thing, then, our emotions change. Our thought life usually precedes our actions. God's love is countercultural.

Some of you have had much more serious issues that may have made it impossible for you to forget. I'm going to tread lightly here and let Dr. Mo give her input at the end of this chapter. I want you to consider transforming the way you think about yourself.

Romans 12:1–2 says, "And so, dear brothers and sisters, I plead with you to give your bodies to God because of all he has done for you. Let them be a living and holy sacrifice—the kind he will find acceptable. This is truly the way to worship him. Don't copy the behavior and customs of this world, but let God transform you into a new person by changing the way you think. Then you will learn to know God's will for you, which is good and pleasing and perfect."

Did you notice the phrase, "but let God transform you into a new person by changing the way you think"? With the power of your own mind, you can allow God to help you. God won't force himself on you. But you can ask him for his help. He will help you to begin to change the way you think. Once we begin changing the way we think about a past emotional wound, we begin to experience a little more freedom and hope for ourselves. This is good news and is a small sample of the power of the gospel of Jesus Christ!

Another principle to help us begin to face painful memory scars is found in Philippians 3. In the first few verses, the writer, Paul, shares his heritage, which is impressive if you are familiar with the Jewish culture. Then he discusses how he gave up everything for Christ.

Next, he says that in order to pursue something—or actually someone—much more powerful than his remarkable lineage and wealth, he had to change his focus. Philippians 3:13–14 explains, "No, dear brothers and sisters, I have not achieved it, but I focus on this one thing: Forgetting the past and looking forward to what lies ahead, I press on to reach the end of the race and receive the heavenly prize for which God, through Christ Jesus, is calling us." This principle is trying to forget the past because, for Paul and for some of us, our past may keep us from experiencing all God has for us in the present and future.

One of my favorite quotes is: "Don't let the pain of your past punish your present, paralyze your future, and pervert your purpose because you have a godly destiny." Gospel preacher Louis Greenup created this quote, and I added to it.

Think about it. If we constantly live in our past and are defeated by it, that in itself can be depressing and hopeless. This is why I believe it is critical that we at least face our past. Bishop Greenup also said, "We need to develop spiritual amnesia."

I'm not suggesting that we forget our past, as that may be impossible, but I believe we should not be held prisoner by our past or memory.

If we aren't careful, we can unintentionally put ourselves in emotional slavery. As a little boy, I was playing on the front porch with Grandma Scales. Another boy with whom I'd just had a fight was walking down our street. My grandma said, "What's wrong with you? You were fine until you saw that little boy." I explained what had happened earlier that morning. Then Grandma Scales said something that I've never forgotten. She said, "That little boy owns you." I was in emotional slavery.

What's emotional slavery? Emotional slavery is when, every time you see someone, hear their voice, or hear their name, you lose it for a few moments, hours, or days. That person owns you. You are in emotional slavery. We'll discuss how to get free from this slavery in our chapter on getting unstuck emotionally.

But think about this: God is willing to help us, but only if we ask him to do so. He does not force us to do anything. Next, we can try to begin to live, not focusing on our past. God is with us, and he is empowering us during our entire journey, so we are not alone, nor are we trying to do it in our own power.

Also, God promises to give us his peace according to Isaiah 26:3: "You will keep in perfect peace all who trust in you, all whose thoughts are fixed on you!"

Consequently, we have the choice and ability with God's help to determine on what we focus. This is great news! Isaiah 26:4 says, "Trust in the LORD always, for the LORD GOD is the eternal Rock." God can be our Rock if we let him.

What if we are nervous about facing our past? We could do what some Old Testament God-followers did. When they prayed, they mentioned the God of Abraham, Jacob, and other patriarchs. By doing this, they remembered what God did for their ancestors in the past. And this seemed to give them the confidence and faith to ask God for their present needs.

Philippians 4:13 says, "For I can do everything through Christ, who gives me strength."

You can win the battle for your mind!

Let's see what Dr. Mo has to say about this.

DR. MO'S COUCH

There indeed is a battle for your mind. And because we know this onslaught is constantly raging, we need to employ unique and specific strategies in this battle. We need to be proactive and have these strategies readily available at our disposal. Clarence has already laid the foundation needed for spiritually engaging in the battle. What I will discuss will be various coping strategies to help while in this battle.

As Clarence was able to determine in his encounter playing basketball, his feelings were based on what he thought about the situation. He thought this encounter was racially motivated. Therefore, he became quite angry. Once he realized the young man was immature and not a racist, he realized his feelings were based on what he *thought*. He then was able to manage his feelings more appropriately. In order for us not to "lose our minds," there are times we have to take pause and evaluate our thoughts. Yes, it may require gathering additional information. It may require us reinterpreting the event. Once Clarence spoke to this gentleman, he realized the guy had no ulterior motives. Without that additional information, Clarence could have continued to ruminate on this encounter and harbored bitterness and anger every time he saw this person. Although he admittedly remembered the incident when he would see this guy, he now could say, "This is my friend," and could move forward with peace of mind. We have to take an appraisal of the situation that is causing us distress. Is it possible to ascertain more information? Will that additional information help us to release rehearsing the hurt? Especially after we determine the event was not as bad as we initially thought?

But what do we do when the additional information confirms what we originally thought? What if Clarence found out the guy was a racist? It would be reasonable to understand why his anger is justifiably intense. How would he negotiate this type of experience to keep from falling into, as he terms it, emotional slavery?

Clarence demonstrated the ability to express his emotions. In some cases, people have been socialized to repress feelings. If we are feeling angry or sad, we need to first and foremost name and express that emotion. Repressing negative emotions is an unhealthy coping mechanism, especially over the course of time. The repressing of emotions can have adverse effects on one's emotional and physical well-being. So it is healthy to name and express the emotion.

Although emotions can be intense at times, we still need to maintain the ability to manage those emotions. However, we have to learn ways to regulate our emotions. Some ways we can regulate our emotions is in choosing to forgive and not harbor anger or indebtedness, reframing negative self-talk, meditation, prayer, and relaxation techniques. This enables us to be in control of our feelings instead of our feelings controlling us.

As Clarence dealt with the addiction to pornography, he realized he had a problem. That's the first step: acknowledging help is needed. He prayed to God for help. And God indeed helped him. Once you determine there is a problem, you begin a process of finding effective ways of dealing with that issue. If you are dealing with a temptation as Clarence did, you must immediately employ other options. And again, being proactive will be more advantageous. Before you find yourself facing the temptation again, think about what those other options will be ahead of time. Will you call a trusted sponsor or mentor? Your therapist? A friend? Walk away? Put the substance or video away? It is more helpful to know what you can do when you are in those situations before you are there.

And of course, as a therapist, I will suggest seeking help from a professional counselor. During

Clarence: "I'm changing because I thought I lost my Fitbit and surprisingly, I had a really good attitude. Normally, I would have been upset. I might have gotten saved when I was in my dark place!"

Dr. Mo: "You are hilarious!!! I hope everyone has made it home. And the Shulers are hunkering in and down for some quality family time! Merry Christmas! You're such a blessing—you and your beautiful family."

Clarence: "I found the book *I Don't Want to Talk About It.* I guess I'll start over reading it. FYI, my last name doesn't have a 'c' in it. We weren't poor, we were 'po' and couldn't afford an extra letter in our last name. Thanks for checking on me. I really appreciate it! Merry Christmas to your family and you."

Dr. Mo: "Really??!!! Couldn't afford the letter??? You really need time to revive your mind Bro! Can't wait to hear your insights on your depression book!! It will be time to roll up your sleeves!!"

Clarence: "Bishopette, did I email you my PowerPoint of 'Biblical Tips for When You're In a Dark Place'? I'm working on 'Necessary Changes After Coming Out of Your Dark Place.' I hope you like it. Thanks again for helping me and continuing to check on me. I must admit, it's scary how well you know me."

Dr. Mo: "The Spirit is truly up to something!! I am excited!!"

those times when the things we have mentioned do not seem to be effective, you may need to try counseling. Clinicians are trained to evaluate if something more could be contributing to your feeling as though you are not winning the battle for your mind. Seek out social support from your family and friends to see if they think you will benefit from professional counseling. Some issues are traumatic in nature and deeply embedded internally. Some may be repressed if you do not readily practice expressing your emotions. These are examples of times you need to consider professional assistance.

The battle is won. Fight from the position of victory.

YOUR JOURNEY

Remember to think about this: God is willing to help us, but only if we ask him to do so. He does not force us to do anything. Next, we can try to begin to live, not focusing on our past. God is with us, and he is empowering us during our entire journey, so we are not alone, nor are we trying to do it in our own power. Let's look at what we covered in this chapter so we can move forward.

- How do you feel about this battle for your mind? Have you thought about it before or is this new to you?

- How do you feel about your past?

- Do you spend a lot of time thinking about your past? Does thinking about your past influence you positively or negatively?

If thinking about your past influences you negatively, what ways does this chapter help you?

1. _____

_____

2. _____

_____

3. _____

_____

- How do you feel about the fact that you have the power to control and even change how you think?

- Does the fact that you have the power to control your mind give you hope? If yes, how so?

- Have you ever thought about the fact that God is with you, so you're not alone in the battle for your mind?

- How do you like the questions to help you determine to whose voice you are listening?

CHAPTER SIX

SIX CHAPTER SIX

GETTING UNSTUCK

*If you want to go somewhere you have never
been before, you must be willing to do something
you have never done before!*
—Alvin Simpkins, senior pastor, Emmanuel Christian Center

Depression, for me, includes mentally wrestling with my thoughts and emotions. Usually, I prefer to be left alone. Frequently, I feel sorry for myself. But often, I don't realize that I'm feeling sorry for myself. From my perspective, my emotions are responding naturally to my observation that I'm being treated or have been treated unjustly. I'm simply trying to survive. I definitely do not want to hear any Christian rhetoric—for example, "When God closes one door, he opens another," or "This is God's will," or "God will make a way out of no way." These statements are true, but when I'm stuck, please just leave me alone and stop talking to me! When I'm stuck emotionally, having a pity party is common. When I'm stuck emotionally, I feel that I'm a failure or I believe that I've been unjustly rejected, especially within the context of racial issues.

What about you? In order to evaluate our situation, we may need to ask and answer a few questions. The first four are:

- Am I stuck emotionally?

- How do I know that I'm emotionally stuck?

- Do I want to get unstuck?

- Will I try to get unstuck?

Do you remember Eve from the "Battle for Your Mind" chapter? Eve seemed to be emotionally and mentally stuck for a moment when she wrestled with Satan. He told Eve that if she ate the fruit of a particular tree, she would become just like God.

Reviewing Eve's story sadly reminds me of me. Remember, I wanted that diversity consulting job with the life-changing money so badly! It seems that both Eve and I (in this case) self-seduced ourselves to the extent that we forgot who we were and whose we were.

Eve wanted to make sure that she wasn't missing out on anything, so when Satan told her that God was holding out on her, she coveted what she already had! Satan told her, "You won't die! ... God knows that your eyes will be opened as soon as you eat it, and you will be like God, knowing both good and evil" (Genesis 3:4–5). What is so incredible to imagine is that in Genesis 1:26, "God said, 'Let's us make human beings in our image, to be like us.'" In Genesis 1:27, it states, "So God created human beings in his own image. In the image of God he created them; male and female he created them." Another definition of the word "image" is the word "likeness." Eve already had God's DNA.

Satan told Eve that if she ate of the fruit from the tree that God commanded her not to eat from, she would be *like* God. It is fascinating reading because Satan tried to give Eve something she already possessed! This is why Satan is called the deceiver.

He doesn't own anything, so he can't give anything away. And he wouldn't give anything good to anyone because that's his nature—evil.

Eve wanted to be like God, and I wanted life-changing money so that I could be my own god. Sadly, tied to this consulting-job money was part of my distorted view of my self-worth. I was seeking self-validation from this diversity consulting job. In my mind, securing this job somehow communicated to me that I had finally "made it." I would now, somehow, be worthy because of the money and this well-known company's reputation in the secular and also the Christian conservative world. This job would give me instant credibility, and probably other Christian organizations would seek me out and pay my fee. I would finally have power and control my destiny! But I would be worthy of what?

I can't speak for Eve, but my battle was with idolatry, the worship of myself. Man, that is ugly!

There is no way to make this pretty. With pornography addiction or other addictions, we can call them diseases or sometimes blame others for our addictions because they may have introduced us to it. But not so with idolatry; it is just plain ugly selfishness.

With both Eve and me, neither one of us trusted God nor, at that particular time, believed God loved us enough to satisfy all of our needs. We wanted to control our own destinies.

I believe that I self-seduced myself into depression; when I didn't get what I wanted, I felt like a failure again, felt betrayed, and felt rejected.

Certainly, I'm not suggesting that all depression is self-induced, just that mine was. My self-seduction and consequent depression were based on a distorted lie about my value, success, and my negative feelings about myself.

How did I get unstuck, or how did I come out of my last depression, my last dark place? I wish I could tell you I was so strong spiritually or that I just prayed and it was gone or I quoted a verse and it was over.

As I mentioned earlier, I needed help! I needed counseling. This was difficult for me because I counsel so many people. So I thought I could counsel myself. I couldn't.

And at this time in my life, I didn't want to do anything.

ACCEPTING A FRIEND'S HELP

I'm going to share some of the texts between Dr. Mo and me. God used her to help me become unstuck from my emotional wound-edness. This is a little unusual, and there are more than a few texts. But it is crucial if you are attempting to help someone wrestling with depression to persevere in pursuing them because often the one being pursued sees it as love and acceptance. Love and acceptance are frequently keys to the door of hope. I'm letting you in on some of Dr. Mo's counseling of me. Pay attention to the dates (for reasons I'll explain later). Dr. Mo heard my cry for help and graciously offered to help me. Once I accepted her help, I slowly began to get better.

"When you're in a dark place, it is also a *sacred* place because God is there with you."

On October 26, 2017, Dr. Mo and I were texting. She immediately got my attention by challenging my thinking. Dr. Mo wrote, "When you're in a dark place, it is also a *sacred* place because God is there with you." That blew me away! I never thought of God being with me in my dark place. I always thought and felt alone. It was a profound statement and gave me hope because now I knew God was with me in my dark place. He never leaves us! This is more good news! But it is one thing to believe this intellectually and quite another to embrace it experientially.

She asked me a question and made a statement to which I responded, "Today, I'm tired of being a Black man in America."

My next response to Dr. Mo was, "Thanks for letting me be honest with you."

She replied, "Thank you for entrusting such a sacred place with me. I appreciate you. That ministered to me." I should have asked her how my situation ministered to her, but I was focused only on me—selfish.

As my session with her concluded, Dr. Mo offered a prayer for me: "I pray you are finding more comfort in your sacred space. May you dwell there until you feel your strength has been renewed."

I thought, *What a prayer! It's okay to stay in my dark place, not rush to get out? God can heal me in my dark place? WOW! Imagine having the freedom now not to pretend or rush to be healed!* Dr. Mo's counseling was so good for me because it was refreshing! She spoke hope and life to me. It took the pressure off. Now I could just wait and listen for God to speak to me in my dark place!

I texted Dr. Mo, "You really helped me. God used you to give me the freedom to grieve in my own way. Thanks so much!" I asked her to repeat the phrase about the dark place being sacred.

She said, "I refer to it as the *sacred place of suffering.*"

Dr. Mo and a few others helped me to evaluate and process my depression and related perspectives. She encouraged me in this process.

Let me share some more communication between Dr. Mo and me; then, I will give some insights that helped me and may help you if you are trying to get unstuck.

Periodically, Dr. Mo would text me articles she thought I should read and process. For example, she sent me Chuck Swindoll's devotional "Contradictory Truths, Part Two."[3] Dr. Mo didn't demand that I read this article; maybe she knew that I didn't like to be told what to do. But she would say something like, "I thought of you when reading this." I couldn't get mad about that. She was extremely sensitive in approaching me for a while, which I appreciated.

I was honest with her: "I didn't enjoy reading this [article], but I needed to read it. This article spanked me. I think God is trying to pull something out of me that I don't want to let go of. Thanks for your prayers, for sharing this article and for being an amazing Christian sister to me! Blessings."

What was so powerful for me was that Dr. Mo consistently checked up on me for almost a year! She didn't just stop once I told her that I had come out of my depression. She'll tell why later.

So didn't I get myself unstuck emotionally? No, I had help.

It is not a sign of weakness to ask for help. For some of us, like I was initially, pride can kept us from asking for help. I desperately needed it, but just didn't know it. She gently pressed me at times to examine myself more than I would do by myself. I was so blessed to have a friend like Dr. Mo who reached out to me.

HELPING A FRIEND
FEEL SAFE

You may not be the one to get your friend emotionally unstuck, but actress Viola Davis shared some practical and helpful tips for a friend possibly struggling with depression on her Instagram account. She says, "There are so many ways to make someone with depression feel loved-no matter whether they feel like talking, go quiet, or socially withdraw." She suggests that when they socially withdraw, you can reach out to them with the following messages:

- "There's no pressure to respond, I just want you to know *I'm here for you whenever you feel up to talking.*"

- "Just so you know—if you ever feel like doing something low key I can come over and we can just watch a movie. *No pressure, I'm here for you though.*"

- "I wanted to reach out to remind you that you're loved ... even in those darker moments when you feel unlovable. *Your depression is lying to you.*"

- "It's okay to take time for yourself—*you've got a lot going on and your mental health matters.*"

- "Just in case you feel bad for withdrawing, please don't. *I know you're going through a lot, I see you.*"[4]

These tips express love with gentleness. These tips are often what a wounded person needs to hear.

MAKING A NON-EMOTIONAL DECISION ABOUT AN EMOTIONAL SITUATION

Also, Dr. Gary Chapman says during his Five Love Languages Marriage Conference, "We have to line up our thoughts with God's Word. Then, we have to line up our actions with the Word of God, then, our emotions will follow. But if we don't change our actions, we will remain stuck emotionally."

One of my practices that keeps me from returning to my pornography addiction is realizing that I have a choice. No matter how strong the seductive powers of the pornography temptation are, I must view it from a non-emotional perspective. It is similar to being a point guard in basketball. A point guard must see the entire floor and even plays developing before they happen.

Spiritually, when I give into this temptation:

- I'll become addicted to it again with all the negative consequences. My eyes and body desperately want to give in to the temptation.

- The Holy Spirit will convict me of my sin.

- I will feel guilt, shame, and like a hypocrite.

- Even after I ask God for his forgiveness, and he forgives me, I will still feel unforgiven.

- It will take time for me to feel better about me. I may struggle with forgiving myself.

- God disciplines me for my disobedience.

I could go on and on. When I view the temptation with all of these consequences in mind, the temptation becomes a non-emotional one. It becomes easier to say, "No."

If you are on medication and you have a counselor, please follow the instructions of your counselor.

For me in regard to my depression triggers, I have the choice to entertain those triggers or to reject them. I use this principle of making a non-emotional decision about extremely emotional triggers. Every time I do this, it makes it easier for me to say "No" to the temptation. Every time I say "No," the temptation's pull grows weaker. This approach helps me to stay unstuck. Or if I get stuck, I can apply this practice to get unstuck. And this practice helps me to stay unstuck!

During the coronavirus, Bishop Courtney McBath said in one of his sermons, "My hope follows my eyes." He seemed to say that how we respond to what we see impacts our hope either positively or negatively. He referred to Philippians 3:12–13: "I don't mean to say that I have already achieved these things or that I have already reached perfection. But I press on to possess that perfection for which Christ Jesus first possessed me. No, dear brothers and sisters, I have not achieved it, but I focus on this one thing: Forgetting the past and looking forward to what lies ahead."

These verses focus on hope and looking forward, which is our choice. Bishop Greenup says, "We need to develop spiritual amnesia and forget our negative past."[5] We may not be able to forget our negative past, but we don't want a negative past to hold us hostage from living and enjoying our present and planning for our future.

Charmas Lee is co-owner with Janice, his wife, of Building Champions, a business that specializes in improving human productivity. They have worked successfully with thousands of individuals in the academic, athletic, and business arenas using their mindset coaching—a high performance mental mastery model that suggests that life is 5 percent psychological and 95 percent physiological. And the 5 percent controls the 95 percent, as argued in his book *Think Say Do*.[6]

This is a fascinating concept and also seems to be a biblical one. So I'm suggesting that we have a voice in our situation. We have a choice. What we focus on mentally will impact our outlook on life. This is exciting and tremendous news!

FACING YOUR FEARS

Another key to getting unstuck is facing our fears. Recently, I had a fear that I owed my old friend, Tim, some money. He'd loaned me five hundred dollars to buy an old car. We'd known each other since high school. I was afraid to call him because it had been years. Maybe because of my cancer or because I was just tired of being a prisoner to my fear, I finally called Tim. He said that I had repaid him. It felt so good to reconnect, and the call alleviated my fear. Facing my fear led me to peace of mind and freedom.

Earlier, I mentioned that the Olympic gold medalist Simone Biles had mental health issues at the Tokyo 2020 Olympics (held in 2021) and withdrew from the competition. What was so amazing during those Olympics was that Simone chose to face her fear! We do have this choice. She won a bronze medal on the beam. But her goal was not to win, but to return to competition. As a gymnast, she knew that some of her events, if done with no confidence or no knowledge of where she is in the air, could literally kill her. She withdrew from most of her events and returned on her own terms. It was implied that counselors on site at the Olympics were meeting with her. Simone Biles won when she decided not to remain stuck. You don't have to remain stuck either. Your recovery may not be as quick as Miss Biles's, but there is no competition here.

Madison Keys is a professional tennis player whose ranking had dropped from being in the top twenty players in the world to fifty-one, but she reached the 2022 Australian Open semifinals. She shared her new mental strategy. She said, "My biggest mindset change is just trying to enjoy tennis, take some of that just internal pressure that I was putting on myself." Keys continued, "It was honestly freezing me. I felt like I couldn't play at all. Just taking that away and putting tennis into perspective: that it's a sport, something that when I was little I enjoyed doing and loved doing it. I was letting it [the pressure] become this dark cloud over me. Just trying to push all of that away and leave that behind last year and start fresh this year."[7]

Jerald January, senior pastor of Vernon Park Church of God, defines discouragement as pressure from the inside. He says, "The greatest enemy of progress is discouragement, and unchecked discouragement destroys dreams. One of the worst things you can do when you are discouraged is to leave the situation alone, thinking it will be all right later. It will be all right if you deal with it because it is like a cancer. It will spread. It needs to be cut out." Pastor January refers to Exodus 6:6. The Israelites did not listen because of their discouragement and cruel bondage. They didn't believe God.[8]

If you have a fear from your past, consider discussing it with a family member or close friend. Think about a way to possibly face your fear. You don't have to face your fear alone.

WHAT DO I REALLY
BELIEVE ABOUT GOD?

More than once, I've asked the question, "Can God really do what he says he can for me?" Now it becomes an issue of faith: What has God done for me lately?

When I review my past, I'm overwhelmingly reminded that God has never failed me! This is so encouraging to me and simultaneously embarrassing. It is inspiring because God hasn't ever failed me, so I can ask him for help. It is embarrassing because God has never failed me—my memory is so short. And, unfortunately, I often take God and his blessings for granted.

Based on God's faithfulness and goodness, I no longer have to prove myself to men. I need to work on remembering his goodness and not taking him for granted.

Let's sit with Dr. Mo for her insight. Then, let's answer a few questions to process what you just read, your time with Dr. Mo, and to help yourself evaluate where you are, why you are where you are, and where to go from there.

DR. MO'S COUCH

Clarence said maybe I'd explain why I continued to check on him after he thought he was better or healed. So I'll share why. You may want to take out your highlighter and illuminate these thoughts so they will always leap out to you. You ready?

I checked on Clarence because I have considered him as a friend. Because I just wanted to support him and check on his well-being. Because I know personally and professionally that depression is a hard thing to battle. It is not impossible, as all things are possible with God (Matthew 19:26). But it is quite a difficult journey.

I checked on Clarence because I wanted to ensure he was really "better." What do I mean? You know how you go to the doctor with, say, a sinus infection? They give you a prescription for antibiotics. On the bottle it will say, "Take all medicine until finished." Because medical professionals know that, once we begin to feel a tiny bit better, we might decide we do not need to continue taking the medicine. Well, I know I'm guilty of doing this.

And then we find ourselves exhibiting symptoms that will suggest the infection is back. Well, it might not be that it is back—it probably never left. Because we so desperately want to feel better, at the first sign we sense improvement, we think there is no reason to take any more medication. I'm better! And we discard the remaining medication. When we needed to take the full course of meds, we toss the notion of needing anything more because we believe we are "all better."

We are indeed improving but may not be quite "all better." Clarence desperately wanted to feel better. "Unstuck," as he says. But as the medical doctors know, if we do not continue the full regimen prescribed, we are susceptible to the symptoms returning, and sometimes with a vengeance. We want to believe we are no longer depressed or stuck or down or whatever our issue might be. And indeed, we can be improving. However, we have to be careful of prematurely abandoning the treatment.

Depression is a hard and difficult road to travel. For some people, it might be more situational and not require a long-term course of treatment. For others, it might be a bit more prominent and require more intensive therapies. And in some cases, depression can be severe. And these cases require highly trained and skilled clinicians and medical professionals working together to provide the best course of treatment possible. Therapy tends to be long term and very intensive in the most severe cases.

I'm very aware of how badly people want to feel better when they have felt awful, when they are in the dark place. It is a scary and lonely and harrowing place to be. Of course, anyone would fight tooth and nail to get himself or herself out. And because of that, there is a tendency to believe one is "all better" when that might not be the actual case yet.

Just as when we go to the doctor to find out what's wrong when we feel bad, we have to get to the root cause of depression. And depending on how long-standing the depression has been, that can possibly determine how long it will take to find out what the culprit may be. Especially when it might be complex and involve numerous factors. And sometimes, we may never get to the "cause." We may be left dealing with and treating only the symptoms.

I wanted Clarence to be cautious. I know too often the excitement of thinking one is finished and no longer needs to continue the prescribed regimen. I did not want to see him plummeting without understanding why that could be the case, especially if he was all better, or so he thought. Sometimes we can resolve issues once we have become aware of the cause, as Clarence discovered. Sometimes we can become aware, and it can send us spiraling downward feeling as though there is no way out. Sometimes we can feel better only to start feeling bad again for a time and then back to

Clarence: "Thanks for the good and timely Word. I just came out of my dark place this morning. Do you have ten minutes?"

About 2 am, I felt like I was wide awake, yet in a dream. God was speaking. There was this incredible peace! It was a very intense worship that I can't put into words. I woke up from this dream or vision to go to the bathroom. When I got back in bed, this dream or vision took up where it left off! This went on until about 4 am. I was changed, no doing of my own! The result of my experience was calm, peace, and a self-satisfaction with myself as I am. God just brought me out of my dark place!

Dr. Mo: "Yes I do."

Clarence: "Do you know a biblical book dealing with depression that you would recommend?"

Dr. Mo: "Try *I Don't Want To Talk About It* by Terrence Real. We can read and discuss it. One of my daughters recommended Briana Babineaux's song 'My Everything.' How are you? How was Thanksgiving?"

Clarence: "I'm very good! God overwhelmed me with His love for more than two hours early this morning!"

Dr. Mo: "That sounds awesome! Had one of those experiences in the wee hours Thursday morning. Did you order the book?"

Clarence: "God revealed that my battle is with idolatry—not pretty, but I'm much better. I'm doing a 20-minute devotional about my experience this Friday morning for the Fatherhood Summit at WinShape, then, I preach about it this Saturday and Sunday. I own that book, *I Don't Want To Talk About It* by Terrence Real. Totally forgot I had it until you mentioned it."

feeling better. It is not as neat and nice as we hope and desire. It can be an up and down, back and forth type of process. That can feel defeating. But we have to know it *is* the journey called depression. When you know what to expect, sometimes you can deal with it somewhat better. Sometimes.

Inasmuch as we want to hurry along our healing, unfortunately it is a process that demands our patience. The society that we live in now deludes us to believe everything can be delivered now. Faster procedures. Delivery services to your door. Hit a button and it's done. It is just not that simple when it comes to our emotional and mental wellness. It takes time.

We tend to become stuck in an emotional place, as Clarence did, when we might not recognize how we are feeling or why we are feeling some kind of way. We can also become stuck when we choose to ignore or not to acknowledge what we are feeling. As I stated in the texts with Clarence, you cannot heal what is not revealed. Clarence recognized he was seeking validation. He recounted times of feeling worthless, rejected, and less than. He had to recognize his feelings and why. So the first thing we have to do is slow down long enough to pay attention to what emotions we are experiencing. We then we have to ask ourselves to what those emotions are connected.

Once we start to connect our emotions with certain experiences, we can begin the process of healing. However, if we choose to ignore our feelings with sayings such as, "That's in the past," or "It doesn't matter," or "I don't really care," we are just suppressing what it is that we are indeed feeling. And, like a pressure cooker, we can only suppress for so long. Those emotions will manifest. Perhaps they come in the intensity of whatever is the emotion being expressed at a given moment. Sometimes suppressed emotions can also manifest somatically. Sooner or later, the top will blow off the pressure cooker if the pressure continues to build.

Mounds of evidence now exist that report the long-term health effects related to unresolved emotional traumas. As the old saying goes, "An ounce of prevention is worth a pound of cure." If we would just acknowledge our feelings, we can prevent much more damage to others and ourselves.

When a car is stuck in the mud, we have to provide some sort of traction between the tire and mud. If no traction is provided, the tires will continue to spin around. The car will remain stuck.

We will remain stuck emotionally if we do not find some traction to get us moving. Sometimes we can pull ourselves out, if we are not too far in. Sometimes a friend can help us. And then there are those times we may have to seek out professional assistance if we remain stuck after several attempts to become unstuck. We may be in deeper and need to seek counseling to help us become unstuck.

YOUR JOURNEY

As you survey the questions below, remember we have a voice in our situation. We have a choice. And what we focus on mentally will impact our outlook on life. This is exciting and tremendous news! There are actions we can take, like reaching out for help, that can aid us in getting unstuck.

- If you've been stuck emotionally in the past, how did you feel?

- How did you become aware that you were stuck emotionally?

What did you do for help? Did you try to get help? If you didn't seek help, what did you do?

1. _____

_____

2. _____

_____

3. _____

_____

- Have you ever gotten past the symptoms of your depression to the root of it?

- If you are depressed and want to get unstuck, will you accept help?

- If you are depressed and emotionally stuck, what would be the first thing you'd do if you got unstuck? Why?

- Have you ever found your own "sacred place of suffering" and let God meet you there?

- What do you think of the possibility of staying unstuck?

CHAPTER SEVEN

GRIEVING AND DEPRESSION: IS THERE A DIFFERENCE?

S ome years ago, when Dennis Rainey and Bob Lepine co-hosted the radio program *FamilyLife Today*, they graciously interviewed me for a couple shows regarding my newest book at that time, *Single and Free to Be Me*. Being with these two men is always fun! But you have to be careful because both of them are extremely quick-witted! All three of us, along with our wives, were on the speaker team of FamilyLife Weekend to Remember Marriage Getaway Conferences. So we knew each other pretty well.

Dennis and Bob asked me about my single life, my previous eleven-year pornography addiction, and my marriage. I expected tough questions about those areas in my life. And they did ask questions about these areas.

But as the last show was coming to its conclusion, just before the last commercial break, Dennis looked at me and said, "You talk about your dad and his hard work to support your mom, your sister, and you in your book *Winning the Race to Unity: Is Racial Reconciliation Really Working?* I know he died when you were twenty years old. What would you want to say to your dad if he were here today?" I was stunned by this question. Tears began to come to my eyes. Dennis's eyes welled up as he looked at my reaction. Fortunately, this show was being recorded. Dennis told me to take a break and come back.

Immediately, I bolted to the men's restroom. I wept. I couldn't stop the tears.

Dennis came into the men's restroom to console me.

Back in the room after a ten-minute break, with tears still in my eyes, Dennis says, "Before we went to commercial break, I asked you what you would say to your dad if he were here today. I could tell by your reaction that it was a very emotional question for you." By this time, the audience in the galley had tears in their eyes, as did the radio technician. Even my male friends who heard this broadcast later called me to tell me that they wept. I answered Dennis's question. My answer was one of honoring my father, who was and is one of my heroes to this day.

What brought about all my emotion was this: When my dad died, I was twenty years old. My mom and sister were so devastated by Dad's death that I focused totally on taking care of them. Gary and Karolyn Chapman and the late Dr. Mark Corts flew back from the Southern Baptist Convention to attend the funeral. Gary and Karolyn sat with us. They were family. Dr. Corts spoke at Dad's funeral.

It all seemed like a blur. All I remember was making sure that Mom and Jean were okay before I returned to Moody Bible Institute. I stayed home an extra week before returning to school.

Once I returned to school, I had to catch up on all my missed assignments and still deal with the racial prejudice at this Christian conservative school. I had a lot of acquaintances because I played basketball for the school team, the first African American to do so. But I only had one close friend, a girl who I took out occasionally. I couldn't wait to get back to talk to her about Dad. But when I got back to school, she told me her dad said that she could no longer see me because I was Black. The only thing I could think of was that she liked me more than I realized and must have told her dad about me. She had agreed to be my date for the school's spring banquet (similar to a prom). She told me she could not go with me. This rejection due to my skin color was part of my Moody experience. There was a constant yet subtle racism that permeated this campus' culture.

God graciously provided three girls, who were roommates at Moody, who took turns taking me on walks to talk. I didn't say much, but it meant so much that they cared. Their actions and cards were such a gift from God. One card that the three of them wrote together, I kept for thirty years until it finally fell apart.

What made Dennis's question so difficult for me is that I realized that I had never grieved over the loss of Dad. I took care of Mom and Jean. I asked Dr. Chapman to take care of them while I was away at school. Once I got back at school, I returned to my routine of survival and work. I never took time to grieve for Dad. Maybe I didn't even know how to grieve or that I should.

For forty years, I had not grieved for Dad. Dennis's question gave me a chance to say "Good-bye" to Dad. God used Dennis to give me permission to grieve. It was incredibly powerful. My tears were tears of joy and release. The emotional weight that left my body was indescribable! I felt so light that I felt that I could dunk a basketball again! Then, I realized that I had unknowingly been carrying this emotional weight for forty years! I had stuffed my emotions about Dad and forgot about my pain and uncertainty. Now, I was finally free of it! I also realized that I was never designed to carry this weight. I had never gone to God to ask if I could give it to him to carry.

> "God used Dennis to give me permission to grieve. It was incredibly powerful. My tears were tears of joy and release. The emotional weight that left my body was indescribable!"

Both grieving and depression are similar in that, in most cases, both are the result of some kind of pain. Both can make us emotionally abnormal and even, in some situations, antisocial. Both can have similar triggers. They both can last a long time.

Dr. Mo will help us with her insight when we go to her couch at the end of this chapter.

As a layperson like many of you, from my perspective, it seems that grieving can lead to depression. Depression seems to be more of a state of mind.

In grieving for my dad, when I finally did grieve, it was a release. It was a release that I didn't even know that I needed. I've always missed Dad and always will. We weren't close emotionally until the last year and a half of his life. He worked so hard to support us. I was extremely lazy and committed only to basketball.

Two years after I became a Christ follower, God allowed me to introduce Dad to Jesus Christ in a personal relationship. We began to grow close. The last time I was with Dad, we prayed together. I was so looking forward to really getting to know him and what made him tick. I wanted him to teach me how to be a man.

Grieving is not about getting over someone or something. It seems to be more about learning how to work through whatever our source of grief is. This is essential if we are to not be slaves to our past and be able to function to our potential in the present.

While it is certainly not a sin to be depressed, depression is something that we may want to view with an attitude of working through it or getting over it. We may never get over the source of our depression, especially if the source is a loved one. But staying in a state of depression is not healthy. Maybe we can view depression the same way that we would a cold. We may have caught a cold at an outdoor football game. If we were at this football game with our father, mother, sibling, or special friend, maybe there are special memories. We never want to forget those special memories, but we do want to get rid of our cold.

It's hard to separate your thoughts about grief and depression. They obviously can be connected, but you need to be clear about the differences.

DR. MO'S COUCH

Yes, there is a difference between grieving and depression. Grieving is a process. Depression can be a state or a feeling. While grieving, we may feel depressed. And sometimes feeling depressed indicates there is a need to grieve.

Most of us as individuals suppress our feelings. Especially when it comes to loss. And death. We usually tell ourselves we have to keep moving. As Clarence stated, when his father passed away, his first thought was to take care of his mother and sister.

We, as a society, rush through most things. We rush through traffic lights. We rush through our meals. We rush through our conversations. We are easily irritated if we are made to slow down. Especially to feel. Especially when those feeling are not the "good" ones.

As Clarence experienced, grief goes nowhere. Just because we do not process and express it does not mean it dissipates into thin air. Most of us will do as Clarence did; we busy ourselves to not deal with those feelings. Other ways people may tend to "deal" by not dealing is to engage in relationships, consume alcohol or other substances, or bury themselves in school or work or some other activity. Anything that numbs the feeling. Anything that silences the voice of the internal turmoil.

If you recognize you've stuffed your depression or grief, you can start right now. It starts with a decision to face and deal with the hurts and pains. No, it's not a pleasant work. But it is a necessary work. When we experience losses in life, especially of our loved ones, it is a natural and appropriate response to cry. Or to be sad. Or mad. Or depressed. Or confused. Irritated. Numb. So many emotions that swirl through us all at one time. But we must do the painstaking work of teasing through those feelings.

If not, there will be a trigger, probably when you least expect it. Clarence did not expect that forty years later he still needed to grieve the loss of his dad. But he did. Because he never did. It was obvious in his case. Sometimes it is not so obvious. If you realize you suppress your feelings, perhaps you can start by talking with a trusted family member or friend. For some, it might require working with a professional counselor. A counselor can help you work through using denial as a means of coping and give you better skills to cope. Also, working with a counselor can unearth years of suppressed feelings. Depending on the nature of the experience, it might be best to conduct that work with a professional.

YOUR JOURNEY

In this chapter we talked about grieving and depression and their similarity that, in most cases, both are the result of some kind of pain. Both can have similar triggers. They both can last a long time. Now it's time to explore what grieving looks like for you.

- How do you define grieving?

- How do you define depression?

- Have you ever stuffed or delayed grieving for someone or about something? Why?

- How did stuffing your grief work for you? Could family or close friends tell?

- Have you ever tried to hide or stuff your depression? Why?

- How did attempting to hide your depression work for you?

Have you ever done as I did in that, after a funeral or some loss, you got so busy trying to survive life that you stuffed your emotion and never realized that you never dealt with it? Identify things that came between you and dealing with your loss.

1. _____

_____

2. _____

_____

3. _____

_____

- If so, what was it? What caused you to stuff it? How did that work for you?

- If you have not dealt with it, do you think you can begin unpacking it now? If not, why not?

- Do you have a family member or close friend with whom you can unpack your grief or depression that you have stuffed for years?

CHAPTER EIGHT

T

IN YOUR DARK PLACE,
GOD IS THERE WITH YOU

When you're in your dark place as a Christ follower,
God is with you, so you're not alone and never alone.
—Dr. Monique Gadson, PhD, LPC

Several factors contributed to my depression. One of the factors was the loss of one of my spiritual mentors, the late Bob Cook. For twenty-three years, I spent time with Bob, usually weekly. He poured into me. Frequently, he introduced me to people he knew such as National Football League Hall of Famer, former Chicago Bear linebacker, Mike Singletary, and the late Chuck Colson. Bob said, "I want you to learn from them so you can help other people." Bob also taught me a lot about being a dad and a husband. Bob was ninety-two when he went to be with the Lord in heaven. I miss Bob.

Before I met Bob, God brought Dr. Gary Chapman into my life; this was before I was a Christ follower and before Gary became famous. God used Gary to introduce me personally to Jesus Christ. God has given me Dr. Gary Chapman as a spiritual dad. He has always been there for me.

God also gave me the late John Bass, Gordon Loux, and Dr. William Pannell. All of these men either have or are serving as father figures or mentors for me.

But I would dishonor my father, Clarence Shuler Sr., if I don't mention him. He worked two or three jobs to make sure we had food on the table, but my dad never told me he loved me. That was a difficult issue for me for many years.

I remember complaining to Mom about Dad after he had left for work: "Dad doesn't love me!" I had just made the All-Star basketball team and won a trophy for shooting the highest free throw percentage for fifteen-year-olds at the Wake Forest Basketball Camp. And I was the only camper who received a standing ovation from the other three hundred basketball campers when I received my trophy from the late Jack McCloskey. Dad bought me a Coca-Cola at the campus. The guy who served me the Coca-Cola asked Dad, "You must be proud of him?" Dad nodded affirmatively, then took me home. He didn't say anything about one of the most memorable nights of my young life!

Mom was a student of her husband. She was not going to let me speak negatively about her husband. She said, "Your father does love you, but he doesn't know how to say it to you. Your grandfather is great with you, giving you all kinds of affection. But your grandfather never told your dad that he loved him." My grandfather emotionally wounded my dad by never telling him that he loved him. Mom went on to tell me how my dad would sneak into my basketball games to see me, but not let me see him. She told me of so many other things he did as well.

Through Mom, I indirectly received my dad's blessing. My second year at Moody, Dad wrote me a letter. It read, "Saw a young preacher today. He reminded me of you. Keep the Faith." This was as close as my dad ever came to saying he loved me. I kept rereading his letter until it literally fell apart in my hands.

Why am I telling you this? I don't want you to jump to conclusions about a relative that you may feel rejected you. Especially if you don't know the entire story from someone who loves you and you trust! It would be so easy to assume someone rejected you and for you to carry unnecessary baggage for years. This could be a contributor to some of your depression.

FRUSTRATED WITH GOD

While working through my depression, I stumbled upon Psalm 27:13, "I would have lost heart, unless I had believed that I would see the goodness of the LORD in the land of the living." This version is from the New King James Version of the Bible. This psalmist seems to believe that even in the midst of his dark place, God is going to do something good for him right here on earth in the future.

It might surprise you that there are people in the Bible who were frustrated with God. One of these people is Jeremiah. Jeremiah, in layman's terms, today would be considered a preacher. So think about it: a preacher, a servant of God, a man of God got frustrated with God! In Jeremiah 20:7–18, Jeremiah vents to God about his frustration with God. Verse seven reads, "O LORD, you misled me, and I allowed myself to be misled. You are stronger than I am, and you overpowered me. Now I am mocked every day; everyone laughs at me."

Here's what we can learn from Jeremiah's complaint:

- God's grace is greater than we can imagine. In verse 7, Jeremiah calls God a liar. If I had been God, I would have zapped Jeremiah right then and there. But God is much more gracious than most of us.

- Jeremiah was talking to God, not about him. He was not gossiping about or slandering God.

- Jeremiah was talking to the God who could change his circumstances or change him.

- Jeremiah got as close to crossing the line with God as possible. (It's not our initial response but the end result that is important to God.)

- Telling God how we feel isn't necessarily attacking his character.

- We might as well be honest with God because he knows our thoughts anyway: "And I, because of their actions and their imaginations, am about to come and gather all nations and tongues, and they will come and see my glory" (Isaiah 66:18a NIV1984).

- God tests those he has made righteous in hopes of spiritual promotion (for Satan, other Christ followers, and non-believers to see how we who profess him respond to adversity). "O LORD Almighty, you who examine the righteous and probe the heart and mind, let me see your vengeance upon them, for to you I have committed my cause" (Jeremiah 20:12 NIV1984).

- We can't deny the goodness of God—it is like "fire shut up" in our bones; we can't keep it in. "But if I say, 'I will not mention him or speak any more in his name,' his word is in my heart like a fire, a fire shut up in my bones" (Jeremiah 20:9 NIV).

GOD'S WORD GIVES LIFE

Dr. Mo's statement, "When you're in your dark place as a Christ follower, God is with you, *so you're not alone* and *never alone*," was crucial in my getting unstuck.

Then, I found this verse in the Bible, Isaiah 43:2, which reads, "When you go through deep waters [a dark place], I will be will with you. When you go through rivers of difficulty, you will not drown. When you walk through the fire of oppression [or depression], you will not be burned up; the flames will not consume you."

When I turned sixty years of age, there were two things that I wanted to do because I lived in Colorado: (1) go whitewater rafting and (2) go fly-fishing.

My church went whitewater rafting. Unfortunately, Brenda and I were put in a raft with the least experienced group. Some of the folks in our raft did not paddle as instructed by our guide. This resulted in our raft hitting a rock and my falling out of the raft into the river that was twice as high as normal and twice as fast. So this Isaiah 43:2 verse resonated with me and still does. I remembered the guide's instruction as to what to do so that I didn't drown. Though even humanly alone under the water, I was not alone because I had the guide's voice and instruction in my head; it saved my life!

"In the darkness, God—who knows our name—wants to establish a deeper intimacy with us! And because his treasures and riches are in this darkness, there is no need to rush out of the darkness."

God will save us too if we follow his instructions.

THE BENEFITS OF THE DARKNESS

Who would think that there could be a blessing from God in our dark place? Dr. Mo is right that our dark place is a sacred place because God is there with us. We are not alone. Isaiah 45:3 says, "And I will give you treasures hidden in the darkness—secret riches. I will do this so you may know that I am the LORD, the God of Israel, the one who calls you by name." There are hidden treasures and secret riches in the darkness! In the darkness,

God—who knows our name—wants to establish a deeper intimacy with us! And because his treasures and riches are in this darkness, there is no need to rush out of the darkness or fake being fine. There can be rest and refreshment in our dark place as God teaches and heals us.

"The LORD will guide you continually, giving you water when you are dry and restoring your strength. You will be like a well-watered garden, like an ever-flowing spring. Some of you will rebuild the deserted ruins of your cities. Then you will be known as a rebuilder of walls and a restorer of homes" (Isaiah 58:11–12). God can become our primary caretaker during our time in the darkness or the desert. God will use some of us once he has built us up to help others to be rebuilt or be restored from their dark place.

It is when we help others in our place of woundedness or weakness that it becomes much more difficult for us to relapse in that area out of which we came. These last two verses are so full of priceless truths about God as he restores and rebuilds our lives.

For me, knowing that I'm never alone brings me peace of mind and comforts my soul. My dear friend Bob Hudson, the founder and director of Men at the Cross, says this: "The idea that God isn't with you in your dark place is an illusion." Ephesians 1:13–14 reinforces this truth: "In Him, you also, after listening to the message of truth, the gospel of your salvation—having also believed, you were sealed in Him with the Holy Spirit of promise, who is given as a pledge of our inheritance, with a view to the redemption of God's own possession, to the praise of His glory" (NASB). Paul is referring to the promised Holy Spirit that Jesus Christ talked about in the Gospels before he returned to heaven. The Holy Spirit indwells every person who asks Jesus Christ to forgive them of their sins and come to live in their lives. God himself in the person of the Holy Spirit lives in us continuously, so we are never alone!

What else can we learn about being in a dark place? As mentioned earlier, God is with us in our dark place:

- Since God is with us in our dark place, our dark place *can be* a holy place or a sacred place of suffering, as Dr. Mo says. Our experiencing this fact depends on our relationship with God. We may miss the holiness of this dark place if we don't embrace God while we are there.

- God heals us in our dark place because we can't come out of our dark place without him. Some of us may suppress our pain and still be able to function. But without allowing God to heal us, we'll continue to carry the pain of our dark place.

- God may need to kill something in us, which may have been beneficial before in order to birth new life for something else better he wants to do in us and possibly through us for his glory. Jeremiah 18:4 reads, "But the jar he was making did not turn out as he had hoped, so he crushed it into a lump of clay again and started over."

- We need to be able to distinguish the difference between *self-pity* and *grieving* (only God and you know the difference—ask him for clarity).

HOW GOD GOT ME OUT OF MY DARK PLACE

After being passed over for the big job, I was in as deep a depression as I could remember. I was so disappointed. I felt like my chance for big-time success and money was gone forever. I didn't want to let my guard down again and to hope, only to be disappointed again.

God was able to get me out of my depression. How did he do it? First, I cried out for help, not very loudly, in my ministry newsletter. Dr. Mo heard my cry and responded.

Next, my old Microsoft Outlook program didn't allow me to inform people that I was out of the office. So people kept contacting me for help. Thus, I kept serving others, similar to Joseph in the book of Genesis in chapter 40. Joseph, while in prison for a crime he didn't commit, helped the chief cupbearer and the baker, both of whom Pharaoh had put in prison. Helping these two men helped Joseph's time in prison go a little faster. And helping others distracted Joseph from his own dilemma. Eventually, God used the chief cupbearer to get Joseph out of prison.

Another factor that God used to get me out of my dark place were the godly friends who kept checking on me, primarily Dr. Monique, Johnny Parker, and Jonno Strickling.

Being in my dark place gave me a better understanding as to why some Christians, including me, don't respond immediately to a biblical truth or counseling. Christians may recognize the truth or counseling insight. But the pain may be so great that it just takes time for an individual to process it. Or it takes time for the emotional and the mental aspects in the brain and heart to get on the same page. There's not necessarily a timetable for emotional healing. But you don't want to stay emotionally wounded forever.

One factor that God used—by which I was completely blindsided—was the fact that one of my clients, who was going through a difficult divorce, helped me. He told me about the church he attended. It emphasized that in the Bible, the people in the stories were not the heroes or stars of the story. They were only part of the story, just like we are part of God's story. The story is about God. This was so helpful to me because I struggle with self-worship.

As God revealed this to me, I remembered Stephen Kendrick's prayer for me before I went in to make my diversity presentation to this multi-billion-dollar organization. Stephen prayed for God's will to be done. Possibly all God wanted to say through me to those executives was said in my presentation. It took me a while to get to this kind of thinking.

Another practice that I continued, which I would not have done if I had not been married to Brenda, was to go to church. There was no way she was going to let me stay at home alone and mope by myself. Every Sunday, my pastor would say something that I could hang on to for the upcoming week. I don't remember the exact sermons, but the truths in the sermons resonated with me. For me, most of the truths that I resonated with were subpoints.

One thing I did not do, but wished I had, was to thank God before you or your circumstances are changed (see Psalm 57:3–7).

First Thessalonians 5:17 says that I should thank God for things not going the way I wanted them to go. Wow, what a concept!

God used all of these factors to get me out of my dark place, but they didn't happen all at once.

Another critical truth is that we need to be able to distinguish between self-pity and grieving (only God and you know the difference—so ask God for clarity). I'm repeating this truth because it is crucial for us in turning to the light while we are in a dark place.

HURT PEOPLE TEND TO HURT PEOPLE

Have you heard the phrase, "Hurt people tend to hurt people"? I found this phrase in the title of an article by Marriage Mission International in the 2018 May/June issue of *Rescue*.[9] The article listed fifteen tendencies of hurt people. Hurt people:

- Often transfer their inner anger to those around them.

- Interpret every word spoken to them through the prism of their pain.

- Interpret every action through the prism of their pain, causing them to suspect wrong motives or evil intent.

- Often portray themselves as victims and have a "victim spirit."

- Often alienate others and wonder why no one is there for them.

- Have the emotional maturity of the age they received their [un-dealt-with or unhealed] hurt.

- Are often frustrated and depressed because past [unhealed] pain continually spills over into their present consciousness.

- Often erupt with inappropriate emotion because words, actions, or circumstances "touch" and "trigger" past [unhealed] wounds.

- Often occupy themselves with busyness, work, and/or accomplishments as a way of compensating for low self-esteem.

- Often attempt to medicate themselves with excessive entertainment, drugs, alcohol, pornography, sexual relationships, or hobbies as a way to forget their pain and run from reality.

- Have learned to accommodate their private "false self" or "dark side."

- Are often self-absorbed with their own pain and are unaware they are hurting others.

- Are susceptible to demonic deception (there is a spiritual battle for your mind).

- God often purposely surfaces pain so hurt people can face reality.

- Need to forgive to be released and restored to freedom.

These fifteen tendencies provided me with so much insight, not only into myself, but for others such as family members, peers, and clients. These tendencies brought clarity to some people's actions. It helped me to be more sensitive and understanding.

The first three points demonstrate that often when we have not been healed from our hurt, our focus is usually more on ourselves than others. So our misdirected focus may result in our blaming others for our situation and/or being angry with others when, in reality, we may be mad with our situation or ourselves. Unfortunately, sometimes we may refuse to take responsibility for a situation we may have caused. We may be unintentionally selfish and not realize it, but those around us can.

Maybe when we are hurt, we tend to hurt those who are closest to us because they are usually the only people who will tolerate our unjustified actions directed at them.

The tendency is for a hurt person to have the emotional maturity of the age they received their [un-dealt-with or unhealed] hurt. This clearly explains why some people get stuck and can't move on without help.

From a spiritual perspective, I found it quite startling and dangerous that our depression or being stuck can open the door in some cases for demonic deception. Remember the chapter about the battle for your mind? Satan may be telling you that you're no good, which is a lie.

In the midst of this spiritual battle, God loves us so much that he will often intentionally bring our pain to the surface so we can face it. We talked about this earlier, that facing our fears and/or depression in some cases can defuse it or can be a first step toward our emotional healing. Again, it is about making a choice. Maybe making a choice is just as critical as knowing that you have a choice!

The last tendency is key: we may need to forgive to be free. We forgive without waiting to be forgiven. When we don't forgive, we hold ourselves hostage. We are the ones holding ourselves in emotional slavery. The first step out of emotional slavery is forgiving those who hurt you. It doesn't imply that or require you to become best friends. Does this sound familiar? It should. Our unforgiveness usually doesn't hurt the other person.

As I study these fifteen tendencies of hurt people, it seems that when we are hurt, we often only focus on ourselves and not those around us. This is not healthy for us or those around us. Often, this is unintentional. We just may not know any better. Or we are so wounded that we may not know for a while how to control the pain we are experiencing.

My friend Dr. Johnny Parker, who calls me his "Big Bro," wrote the book *Turn the Page: Unlocking the Story Within You*. It is an incredible book because it allows you to go at your own pace to examine your life, from the front stage (your public life) to your backstage (your private life). Johnny created a T-shirt to go with it. The front of this T-shirt reads, *"Success Is Hard Work, Heart Work, Worth The Work, Do The Work."* I love it, and it is so true! Whether you have a counselor and read a book like *Turn the Page*, you and your circumstances can be changed with hard work and heart work. It may be scary, but it is definitely worth it, plus it beats your present situation!

One of God's truths to help us when we struggle with feeling sorry for ourselves is found in 1 Corinthians 10:13, which says, "The temptations in your life are no different from others experience. And God is faithful [that's the key]. He will not allow the temptation to be more than you can stand. When you are tempted, he will show you a way out so that you can endure." God will never give us more than we can handle, but he may give us the max that we can handle. And we were never designed to handle things alone without his help. Sometimes, we're trying to carry things only God can carry.

Journaling is an excellent therapy for most people. Journaling often gives you clarity because it turns your gray thoughts into black and white, something concrete beyond emotion when you put it on paper.

Consider journaling your emotions while in your dark place. Then, continue journaling while you are in the process of coming out of your dark place. When you are completely out of your dark place, journal about that too. Next, journal about what God may have taught you during each step of coming out of your dark place. Your journals will be priceless to you, and you may help others with what you learn about God and yourself.

Clare Boothe Luce, former US ambassador, politician, and author, said, "There are no hopeless situations; there are only men [and women] who have grown hopeless about them."

Second Corinthians 1:4–5 reads, "He comforts us in all our troubles so that we can comfort others. When they are troubled, we will be able to give them the same comfort God has given us. For the more we suffer for Christ, the more God will shower us with his comfort though Christ." Thus, sometimes God may allow us to suffer not just for our sake, but so that we may know how to help others who suffer after we've come out of our dark place. So our being in our dark place is not just about us.

One of the truths that I learned is that when God allows us to suffer, it is to show us that our survival is not based on anything we can do, but solely on his grace and power.

James 1:2–4 says, "Dear brothers and sisters, when troubles of any kind come your way, consider it an opportunity for great joy. For you know that when your faith is tested, your endurance

[Christlikeness] has a chance to grow. So let it grow, for when your endurance is fully developed, you will be perfect and complete, needing nothing." What a comforting thought, that being in our dark place is not for nothing and that we will be better on the other side. But we may need to go through our dark place in order to get better and stronger.

Sometimes, God may allow us to go through a dark place not because of our lack of faith, but because of our faith! In the Old Testament book of Job, God bragged on Job's integrity and faith. God wanted to show Job off to Satan. Job 1:8–12 states:

> Then the LORD asked Satan, "Have you noticed my servant Job? He is the finest man in all the earth. He is blameless—a man of complete integrity. He fears God and stays away from evil."
>
> Satan replied to the LORD, "Yes, but Job has good reason to fear God. You have always put a wall of protection around him and his home and his property. You have made him prosper in everything he does. Look how rich he is! But reach out and take away everything he has, and he will surely curse you to your face!"
>
> "All right, you may test him," the LORD said to Satan. "Do whatever you want with everything he possesses, but don't harm him physically."

God initiated Job's suffering by giving Satan permission to test him. All of Job's children were killed, and he lost all of his wealth. In Job 2:6, God gave Satan permission to take away Job's health.

God so strongly believed in Job's faith and that Job would never reject God. Job never rejected God. God provided more children and restored his wealth.

Not only does God want us to be stronger, but he seems to want us to do the impossible as humans. Read what God says in Jeremiah 12:5: "If racing against mere men makes you tired, how will you race against horses? If you stumble and fall on open ground, what will you do in the thickets near the Jordan?" A former Army scout during the time of the Apache Chief Cochise allegedly said that the First Nation people (Native Americans) could run as far as their horse could in one day, naturally not as fast though. But if that is true, then it is not far-fetched to suggest that we could run as far as a horse. Sounds crazy, doesn't it, but it could be possible. The bottom line is that God isn't done with us yet. God may be using our dark place to make us tougher and stronger for his purposes for us. God wants to do great things to us, for us, and through us!

Here are some more verses to help us while we're in our dark place and when we're out of our dark place:

- Romans 5:3–4: "We can rejoice, too, when we run into problems and trials, for we know that they help us develop endurance. And endurance develops strength of character, and character strengthens our confident hope of salvation."

- Isaiah 54:17: "No weapon turned against you will succeed. You will silence every voice raised up to accuse you. These benefits are enjoyed by the servants of the LORD; their vindication will come from me. I, the LORD, have spoken!"

- Isaiah 41:10: "Don't be afraid, for I am with you. Don't be discouraged, for I am your God. I will strengthen you and help you. I will hold you up with my victorious right hand."

- Isaiah 40:31: "But those who trust in the LORD will find new strength. They will soar high on wings like eagles. They will run and not grow weary. They will walk and not faint."

MUSIC FOR OUR SOUL

The last and critical piece for my coming out of my dark place was Christian music. For me, saturating my mind with God's word is crucial. One way to do that is memorizing Bible verses. A more fun way for me is listening to Christian music. These are the songs that helped me:

- "Survivor" by Mika Morrow

- "Imagine Me & Help Me Believe" by Kirk Franklin from the CD *The Fight of My Life*

- "I Forgive Me" by James Fortune

- "Strong God" by Kirk Franklin

- "My Everything" by Bri Babineaux

- "It Doesn't Matter" by Bishop T.D. Jakes from the CD *He-Motion*

- "Champion & God Got My Back" by TaMyya J

- "Clean" by Natalie Grant

- "Thy Will Be Done" by Hillary Scott & the Scott Family

- "A Great Work," "Increase My Faith," and "Still" by Brian Courtney Wilson

- "Deliver Me (This Is My Exodus)" by Donald Lawrence

- "Created to Win" by Algeron Wright

- "Cycles" and "Make Room" by Jonathan McReynolds

- "God Wants to Heal You" by Earnest Pugh

- "In Spite of Me" and "Break Every Chain" by Tasha Cobb Leonard

- "Surrounded (Fight My Battles)" by Lasha Knox & James Fortune

- "Thank You for It All" by Marvin Sapp

- "I Can Only Imagine" by MercyMe

- "I Trust You" by James Fortune

- "Why Not Me" by Tasha Page-Lockhart

- "Never Alone" by Tori Kelly with Kirk Franklin

- "Deliver Me" by Donald Lawrence[10]

So the next time you battle when you're in a dark place, I hope this chapter will help you by providing a different and hopeful perspective.

DR. MO'S COUCH

Clarence did an excellent job in communicating biblical truths revealing God's perspective when we're in a dark place. I thought his insights were awesome!

No couch time needed today!

Dr. Mo: "Heeeeeeyyy!!! Just checking in on you and yours. How are you coming along?"

Clarence: "Thanks for checking on me. I'm OK. Fighting not to return to life as usual because I know I'm changed. I know I need to spend more time with Jesus. I know I don't know how to give all of me to Him. So today, I've been saying I want more of Him. But He has to show me how ..."

"My project manager for one of my most important books that I'll ever write, told me earlier that she wasn't going to finish what she promised to do in September. I thought all this time she was working on it. So I'm trying to finish the work that she was supposed to do this week. Normally, I would have been so upset with her. I'm very disappointed with her, but I have to love her (not work with her again-wisdom-but love her). This is so not me!"

Dr. Mo: "WOW ... yeah cause I would have been UPSET! Maybe this is a way He's showing you how to receive more of Him. Now your editor is off the scene ... that leaves only ..."

Clarence: "If I hadn't gone through the dark place, I would have responded differently."

Dr. Mo: "Praise God for insights gained!"

One week later.

Dr. Mo: "How y'all doing?"

Clarence: "Continuing to process. Had life-changing time last Friday with one of my mentors, Brian Teel, discussing my dark place. He shared with me that he felt that I'm prophetic in that I speak truth that makes people uncomfortable. He shared Jeremiah 12:5, 'If racing against mere men makes you tired, how will you race against horses? If you stumble and fall on open ground, what will you do in the thickets near the Jordan?' He helped me realize Lordship in a totally different perspective. It felt like a salvation experience!"

Dr. Mo: "WOW!! That would explain quite a bit because it truly is lonely out front. And I agree. You do have the task of speaking straight and narrow truths."

Clarence: "I'm getting freed up!"

Dr. Mo: "Healing!"

YOUR JOURNEY

There are hidden treasures and secret riches in the darkness! In the darkness, God—who knows our name—wants to establish a deeper intimacy with us! And because his treasures and riches are in this darkness, there is no need to rush out of the darkness or fake being fine. There can be rest and refreshment in our dark place as God teaches and heals us.

Before reading this chapter, what has been your response to being in a dark place? Why has this been your response?

After reading this chapter, list a few ways you plan to respond to being in a dark place should this happen to you again.

1. _____

2. _____

3. _____

- Did you relate to any of the tendencies of hurt people? If so, which one or ones? Why is this particular tendency an issue for you?

- What do you think of God saying he is with us in our dark place? How does that make you feel?

- What do you think about all of the Scriptures written to help us deal with our woundedness?

- How do you think journaling could be helpful to you when you are in a dark place or even now, if you are not presently in a dark place?

- Do you have family or a close friend in whom you can confide? If not, will you please consider asking God to give you someone?

- How do you feel knowing that some people in the Bible complained to God when they were in their dark places?

- Please review some of the benefits of being in a dark place.

- Listening to music comforts and often inspires me when I'm in a dark place. What about you? Please listen to some of the songs listed in this chapter.

- What are some of the songs that you listen to when you are in your dark place?

CHAPTER NINE

E CHAPTER NINE CHA
NE CHAPTER NINE C

IF YOU'RE CONSIDERING DEATH BY SUICIDE, PLEASE CONSIDER THE PAIN OF THOSE YOU'LL LEAVE BEHIND

Hope comes from hopelessness. Strength comes in weakness.
And peace is found amid the storm.
—Jeff Boesel, 31 Days for the Kingdom: A Devotional
with Global Impact

I had a great dad, mom, and older sister, Jean, who all loved me. I was the baby of the family, so, yes, I was spoiled. My relatives were all crazy Black folks. We usually had great times when we were together. And they all loved and encouraged me, as did all of our neighbors and community. I had made the high school basketball team even though I was only 5'1" in the tenth grade. I did well academically in the predominantly Black school system. I was popular, but I wasn't the coolest person, even though I was in the group of cool people. Yet suicide was an option I considered when I was sixteen years old.

So why did I consider suicide when there were a lot of reasons to live? At that time, I couldn't see those other reasons for living. I only focused on negative issues.

I struggled with the racism toward Blacks in the '50s, '60s, and '70s in America. It seemed the majority of people of the majority culture/race hated me simply because of the color of my skin. I hated being short, even though I had made the high school basketball team. It seemed my parents were always on me for something that I did wrong or something I needed to do. Even though my older sister and I were very close, she unintentionally made school difficult for me. Jean usually made straight As, with an occasional B. So when her former teachers learned that I was her younger brother, they had great academic expectations. Boy, did I disappoint most of them! Bs were my average grade with an occasional A.

There was my subconscious search for my identity as a teenager; I wanted to be popular, especially with the ladies. Basketball was my attempt to be accepted and get the approval of my peers and girls. It was also, from my perspective, a way to prove my manhood—whatever that was.

I was emotionally wounded and didn't know it.

What about you?

Have you ever had a part of your physical body that was in pain? Did you notice that all your attention went to the wounded part of your body? I think when we are physically hurt, we unintentionally neglect the parts of the body that aren't in pain to focus only on the source of our pain. It is not that we don't care about our other body parts; they just aren't crying out for attention or help like the part of our body that is experiencing pain.

Maybe, as a result of rejection, feelings of inadequacy, loneliness, concerns about our physical body, or ongoing aging issues, we may be crying out for help but feel that no one is listening or responding.

If you're considering death by suicide, you may be like the person having an injured body part who is focusing only on your pain. It is not that you don't care about those around you, but you may feel you are in such pain you can't focus on anyone else but yourself. This is natural and normal, but will you please consider this first?

YOU ARE LOVED MORE THAN YOU KNOW

Before you attempt death by suicide as the way to end your present pain, will you please think about those who you would be leaving behind? So please wait in regard to any suicide attempts.

For the last several years, I have served as a sheriff's chaplain. One of my roles is to ride along with deputies to get to know them so I can serve them. Another of my responsibilities is to serve the community. If someone dies in a home, often a deputy sheriff will request a chaplain. Frequently, I receive a call to help the deputy help the family that has just lost a loved one at home. As a result of these calls, I often see death and those left behind. I try to comfort the family by just being there with them, primarily listening to them as they grieve. Sometimes I pray with the families, if appropriate. It is not uncommon for me to help them with funeral arrangements. And I will have the family meet in one room so that they do not see the coroner take the body of their loved one out of the home. And sometimes, I officiate the eulogy for the family.

"There is no way that you can imagine the pain you will cause to those who love you. They love you more than you realize, even though they may not know how to respond to you."

There is no way that you can imagine the pain you will cause to those who love you by taking your life. They love you more than you realize, even though they may not know how to respond to you. Please don't equate their response—or what you may consider as a lack of response or insensitivity—to them not loving you. They may simply not know what to do with or for you. They may be afraid that they will offend you in some way.

In 2018, pastor Andrew Stoecklein died by taking his own life. His wife, Kayla, wrote this: "Please pray for me and the boys [he had three sons]. I don't know how I am going to face this, I am completely heartbroken, lost, and empty. Never in a million years would I have imagined this would be the end of his story."

If you are struggling with suicidal thoughts or actions, please tell someone, call 911 or the National Suicide Prevention Lifeline at 1-800-273-8255. Please make sure you're not alone, and please call a friend or family member before you make that irreversible decision.

You are loved and valued more than you know!

Do you hear Kayla's pain as you read her comments? Her three boys no longer have a father to raise them or teach them how to become young men. Research shows how critical having a father is. Kayla is empty, not knowing, possibly, how to support her three boys. She is now a single mom. We don't know if she has a job or will have to get one to survive. Few insurance companies pay out for a death caused by suicide.

Very possibly, Kayla's husband, Andrew, wasn't thinking about all of these consequences for his wife and sons. He was focused on his own pain.

If you take your life, your parents or loved ones will somehow feel that they failed you. Their guilt will be overwhelming. It's not an experience that people get over. Most simply endure it. A Wisconsin Longitudinal Study of parents (428 in each group), with an average age of 53 years and an average of 18.05 years after the death of a child, showed that these bereaved parents reported more depressive symptoms, poorer well-being, and more health problems and were more likely to have experienced a depressive episode and marital disruption than did a comparison group of parents that did not experience the loss of their child.

So think about it. After you leave by death by suicide, your parents and other family members will often become depressed. They might not even know that they are depressed. If they don't know that they are depressed, they probably will not get treatment because they won't know they need it.

If your parents are in an unknown depressed state, then it is most likely that they will negatively and unintentionally impact those around them, especially immediate family, like each other and/or your siblings if you have any.

You don't want this for your parents or siblings, do you?

Their guilt over the suicide and their blaming themselves entirely for the suicide of their child affects them negatively mentally. It is not uncommon for parents, siblings, and other family members of suicide victims to develop mental health issues. These mental health problems could possibly exist for years without detection.[11]

Research also reveals that your parents will tend not to take as good care of themselves physically as they used to because of the loss of their child.[12]

And in some cases, marriages deteriorate due the suicide of a child. Some marriages end in divorce because each spouse could have the tendency to blame the other for the loss of a child. They may even feel that they don't deserve happiness because they failed their child.

So before contemplating death by suicide, please consider these negative possibilities that will impact your family and loved ones if you take your life. If you love your family, you wouldn't want to leave them to deal with all of these problems as a result of your taking your life.

It seems when people commit suicide; they seldom have any idea of the emotional damage that they can leave behind for their immediate family, other relatives, and friends. If those who commit suicide could see the emotional aftermath in which they leave their families and loved ones, much fewer people would kill themselves.

Those left behind often experience abandonment issues, lack of closure, and guilt. For some, this guilt may make these survivors feel they could have done something to save their loved one who committed suicide. It may also make these survivors feel guilty for enjoying life.

These are issues those who commit suicide or are considering suicide may not contemplate.

As I mentioned earlier, I considered death by suicide.

I decided not to kill myself—not because I suddenly became brave or accepted by others, but because I didn't want to inflict pain on my body.

GOD IS THINKING
ABOUT YOU

Shortly after deciding to live, I reconnected with Gary Chapman. We had met two years earlier on a basketball court in a church family life center. He seemed to accept me as I was.

There was something different about him. I had watched him like a hawk for two years. On a retreat with Gary and the youth from his church on a Saturday evening, he basically asked me if I was satisfied with my life or was something missing. I felt something was missing.

Gary began reciting a verse from the New Testament book the Gospel of John, chapter 3, verse 16 (ESV). It says, "For God so loved [Clarence] that he gave his only Son, that whoever believes in him should not perish but have eternal life." Even though I was not a Christ follower at the time, I knew that verse because I often heard it quoted in church. I was a "drug baby." My parents "drug" me to church it seemed every time the doors were open. I had not embraced their faith because no one had asked me to invite Jesus Christ into my life.

I knew that verse didn't have my name in it. Gary explained, "When God is thinking about the world, he is thinking about you." He further explained that God simultaneously loves everyone and told me how to have a personal relationship with Jesus Christ.

"I'm sharing this with you because life can get better!"

That night, by faith, I asked Jesus Christ to forgive me for my sins and to come into my life and make it what he wanted it to be.

That night, my life changed forever. I no longer wanted to kill myself. Those thoughts of killing myself never returned!

My first night that weekend, a Friday at this mountain retreat, I borrowed a blanket because I had never stayed in the mountains before. I didn't realize that it got so cold there at night. Even with the borrowed blanket, I was still cold. But that Saturday night after asking Jesus Christ into my life, I'm sure my body was still physically cold. But there was warmth inside of me so powerful that I didn't feel the cold.

Why am I telling you all this?

I'm sharing this with you because life can get better! Sometimes, improvement can be gradual or immediate. Sometimes *help can come from unusual sources!* Who would have expected in 1970, with all the racial tension in the country, that a White pastor would share the love of Jesus Christ with a Black teenager?

So I'm asking you to reconsider death by suicide because: (1) the people who love you so much and whom you love, not to mention people who may love you but know nothing about you, will be tremendously impacted in a negative way by your death; and (2) your life as you know it now will usually get better, especially if you don't know Jesus Christ and ask him into your life. Or if you are already a follower of Christ, then spend more time with him in prayer—find other Christ followers with whom to fellowship. You can share your life with them, and they will become a support group for you—to live life with you.

A dear friend of mine, Bo Jennings, shares about his own life:

> Just realized it's been fifteen years since my second suicide attempt. Fifteen years of finally being properly diagnosed. Fifteen years of using what trained professionals gave me to help fight depression. Fifteen years of freedom from trying to tackle depression on my own. Fifteen years of being okay with not being okay. Yes … I worked my butt off to defeat the death grip depression had on me. But without my amazing family, and terrific friends, and the best mental health professionals ever, I would not be here today.
>
> None of us are alone. There are people out there who care about you. All of us are stronger together than we are apart. Don't ever give up on yourself or others around you. I learned that the hard way … twice. And am glad I'm here to talk about it fifteen years later!

One of my clients said that he is so glad that he changed his mind and didn't take his life because he never would have had his son, whom he loves passionately. He also got remarried after several decades of what he termed a bad marriage. So for more than twenty years, he was in a marriage that emotionally wounded him. But now, he is married to a woman he says is changing his life and helping him to heal from his previous marriage.

The man just mentioned above survived twenty difficult years but didn't want to devastate his son. No one wants to be in a difficult situation for twenty years. But he chose to live because of his son, and now he is experiencing some of the best years of his life!

I believe you can too! Will everything be perfect? No! Nothing or no one is. But life can be a tremendous experience. Please consider giving life another chance.

A phrase I remember reading says, "If you rearrange the letters in 'Depression,' you'll get, 'I Pressed On.' Your current situation is *NOT* your final destination." This phrase, though anonymous, is a critical statement for encouragement.

I'm sure Dr. Mo has some more insights regarding giving life another chance.

DR. MO'S COUCH

Due to the nature and seriousness of this topic, please seek immediate help if you are feeling suicidal. Contact 911 or proceed directly to the nearest emergency room.

Suicide is a complex topic. There are many myths that distort discussions about suicide. Sometimes it is very difficult to determine where to begin. However, let me begin by saying, if you are considering suicide, I'm pretty certain you are feeling alone and hopeless. And I want to say to you: I understand.

There are several reasons, factors, and circumstances that can converge at a given point in time that contribute to someone feeling suicidal. And so, to you I say: I know at that moment in time, it is not easy. All I can say is if you are willing to seek out assistance, there is someone willing to walk alongside you to guide you through one of the darkest moments in your life.

If you are not familiar with resources in your area, you can call the **National Suicide Prevention Lifeline at 1-800-273-8255 RIGHT NOW**. There you will find someone who will be able to speak with you and guide you during a very scary time in your life.

All that Clarence spoke of is true. And I'm sure if you've contemplated suicide, or if you're currently wondering if that's the answer for you, it is hard to think about your loved ones and their feelings. People accuse those who attempt or think about suicide as being selfish. That only adds another layer of heaviness upon someone who is possibly feeling overwhelmed already. That is so far from the truth. Sometimes people *are* thinking of their loved ones. Sometimes they feel people will be better off without them.

No one has access to the recesses and corners of your mind. They *really* do not know what you are feeling or thinking, unless you share it with them.

However, let's give thought to what Clarence said. Is there someone you really do not want to leave? Who do you love unconditionally? Who do you know loves you unconditionally and is deeply concerned about your well-being? Are you afraid of your loved ones finding you? Their feelings of devastation? Do you really want to die, or do you want the pain and hurt to stop? I hope you really do not want to die. I hope you have loved ones who give you reason to live.

I hope you are able to communicate to someone you love and who loves you about how you are feeling without condemnation and judgment. If you are unsure, again, call the **National Suicide Prevention Lifeline at 1-800-273-8255**. If you do not have family members, maybe there's a trusted friend who cares for you who can assist you.

Please contact your medical doctor if you have one. Sometimes medication can be the difference maker for those who are feeling despondent. Sometimes therapy along with medication can turn a person's life around for the better.

If you are a believer, the truth of God's word can feel so distant when you're at your lowest. Where is God when all hell is breaking loose in your life? Where is God when your heart is broken and you can feel the sharp pains literally jabbing your chest? Where is God when you have no hope in the world?

It is hard to grasp onto faith when you feel you're slipping and slipping fast. Imagine you're falling down the side of a mountain and you are trying to hold on to the twigs or blades of grass to break your fall. Life can make you feel that way too. If we believe that God's word is true, that he promises we are never alone as stated in Matthew 28:20—"and remember, I am with you always, to the end of the age" (HCSB)—what do we do with that in times of extreme hopelessness?

As simplistic and cliché-ish as this sounds, we believe. If you've ever been in a severe storm, where the weather is tornadic, you hold on for dear life. Literally. Try to do the next thing: Call a loved one. Call a friend. Call the Suicide Prevention Lifeline. Call a doctor. Get a checkup. Go to therapy. Take a walk. Tell someone how you feel. Make a list of those you don't want to leave. Pray. Believe. Hope against hope. Think of what's before you. How might God be right there?

If you really feel the above things are not working, or that you do not have the energy to do those things, please go to the nearest hospital. God has angels that we are unaware of that are located in unexpected places.

I have often said to numerous clients over the years, I find hope in the fact that they scheduled a session, waited until the appointed time of the session, gave voice to those hard to explain feelings, and went home with nothing more than the conversation shared. And there have been times when that was enough. Enough to go to bed that night. To wake the next day. To determine what might be the next thing other than suicide to do.

You have a choice.

And sometimes, little by little, one step at a time, rays of hope shine upon them. It might not mean all is right in their world as they desire. It might not mean that the threat is gone. It just means they try to do the next thing. And when they find what helps them through the moment, until that tornadic and stormy time has passed by, they are more likely to do those things again. Life truly is lived as a journey that we take one step at a time. Sometimes those steps are light and bouncy. Other times we may feel cemented in place, like we do not want to go on.

What does the next thing look like to you? What does it look like to you to believe that God is with you? How does that determine what you will do next?

YOUR JOURNEY

I believe you can experience some of the best years of your life! Will everything be perfect? No! Nothing or no one is. But life can be a tremendous experience. Please consider giving life another chance.

- How do you feel about yourself and why?

- Do you like yourself? Why or why not?

List some of the things that make you laugh.

1. _____

_____

2. _____

_____

3. _____

_____

- Do you have friends or a close friend with whom you can talk about anything?

- How did reading Kayla's questions and pain after her husband committed suicide make you feel? Why?

- What do you think about the statement that you are loved and more valuable to people than you know?

- If you are like Bo and me, who both contemplated suicide, is there anyone with whom you can talk? Both of us are grateful that we were either unsuccessful or didn't go through with the suicide. If you are having suicidal thoughts, please call someone now.

- Do you remember in this book where I encouraged you to like yourself? Please reread that section. (See chapter one, "Possible Triggers for Our Dark Place.")

- Please also reread how God feels about you.

- What do you think about the possibility that life can get better?

- If you love your family and you don't want to hurt them, if you are considering death by suicide, will you please tell them? They want to know.

- If things aren't good with your family, is there a teacher, guidance counselor, or pastor with whom you can talk?

PRACTICING
NEW
WAYS
OF
BEING

CHAPTER TEN

N TEN CHA
TEN CHAPTER TEN C
T EN CHAPTER

LEARNING TO GIVE
YOURSELF GRACE:
"WHY YOU NEED TO LIKE YOU"

A few months after flunking out of college, I found a job and stayed in Chicago. I was twenty years old. I went home for a summer visit and made friends with John (not his real name), a new guy at my home church in Winston-Salem, North Carolina, who had joined our singles group.

John and I became good friends quickly. We both were short. He felt rejected by the world. I felt that way about my former acquaintances, people I thought were my friends at my former college in Chicago.

We both loved basketball. John asked about coming to Chicago to see a professional basketball game in person. I agreed, and John gave me the money for his ticket. I'm so ashamed to tell you this, but I never bought his ticket. I totally forgot about it until he called asking about the game and details. I also spent his money. I didn't intend to, but I stole his money. Do I have an excuse? No. I was young, dumb, and obviously incredibly self-centered. But none of these are valid excuses.

The next time I was back in my hometown, after a singles Bible study, the girl leading the study, one of John's friends, told me how my actions had devastated him! I was so convicted.

Immediately I called John to apologize and to make restitution. I went to his house with his money and to apologize, but he wouldn't come to the door. He would not talk with me or communicate through a friend. He wouldn't take the money I owed him either.

> "Making things right in no way justified what I did. I also realized that carrying the guilt for which God had forgiven me was unhealthy emotionally."

I had seriously wounded this new Christ follower. I've never seen him since. For several decades, I've tried to contact him to repay him and to ask his forgiveness. I've been unsuccessful.

So what do I do? After more than thirty years, I finally forgave myself. I had asked God for his forgiveness thirty years ago. Why did I finally forgive myself? I realized that I had done all I could do to make things right between John and me. Making things right in no way justified what I did. I also realized that carrying the guilt for which God had forgiven me was unhealthy emotionally.

EXACTLY WHAT IS GRACE?

"Grace" is often defined as receiving what we don't deserve. In a sense, grace could be considered a gift. During the Christmas season, many people give gifts not because the people receiving the gifts deserve them, but because the givers are motivated by love. Love is about giving without expecting or demanding anything in return.

If there are people you love, you have probably given them a Christmas gift. But maybe more significant than giving a gift once a year to those you love, you probably give grace even on a daily basis.

When I think about receiving grace on a daily basis, I think of my parents, who gave me grace as a baby before I even knew it. Think of all the encouragement our families and loved ones gave us—when we took our first steps or our first words. As babies, not only were we probably not aware, but if we had been, there was no way to repay those who raised us for what they did for us.

So if those who love us gave us grace, let's consider giving ourselves grace. That is something they would want for us.

Some of us can be amazing in giving grace to other people yet show no mercy to ourselves.

Does that describe you? If so, read on.

STOP BEATING YOURSELF UP

Some of us are very tough on ourselves. Some of us, due to feeling unpopular, lonely, rejected, or due to aging issues, may be extremely demanding on ourselves. We tend not to give ourselves grace. We easily give other people more grace that we give ourselves.

Maybe it is because we don't believe in ourselves or we have been legitimately wounded and unhealed, resulting in our possible insecurity. Sometimes, if we are insecure, we may feel that we don't deserve anything good for ourselves. Or if our parents have been verbally or physically abusive, we may come to believe that we are not worthy of grace from anyone, including ourselves.

Remember how God sees us? He wants us, so he created us. And because he made us in his image, we have his DNA. Thus, we are wanted. We have value, purpose, and a destiny. We need to accept this concept of self-worth. It is okay and actually healthy to know that we have value. Simultaneously, we must not get caught up in self-worship, which is probably not a problem for us if we are beating ourselves up.

Possibly, you believe you have done something that you think is unforgiveable.

Another crucial factor is that no matter how bad I felt about what I did, I couldn't change my past. Did I get away with something? No, I've never forgotten what I did to John. I no longer feel guilty, but remembering my selfish act doesn't make me feel good. But I no longer beat myself up. I'm forgiven. Were there consequences to my sin? Yes: I lost a friend, John, whom I wounded. I'm sure I hurt his family and his friends. My reputation as a Christian took a justifiably negative hit. John certainly didn't deserve to be the recipient of my selfish actions. Most crucial is that I gave John a distorted view of Christ with my selfishness.

God can forgive me like he says in 1 John 1:9: "But if we confess our sins to him, he is faithful and just to forgive us our sins and to cleanse us from all wickedness." God also says in Psalm 103:12, "He has removed our sins as far from us as the east is from the west." In Isaiah 43:25, God also says, "I—yes, I alone—will blot out your sins for my own sake and will *never* think of them again" (emphasis mine). *Wow*! This is such a powerful and liberating verse!

If I trust God, and he can forgive me, then, at some point, I should accept his forgiveness and forgive myself. And if God is no longer going to think about my sin, maybe I shouldn't either. Not forgiving myself after God has forgiven me may be an unintentional act of pride.

LET YOUR PAST GO SO YOU CAN LIVE IN THE PRESENT AND PLAN FOR YOUR FUTURE

If you and I are going to learn to give ourselves grace, then we have let go of our past. Letting go doesn't mean forgetting or that there is not responsibility or accountability. How do we let go of our past? I believe it is an act of our will. Some people say the Bible says to forgive and forget. The Bible does tell us to forgive, but it doesn't say anything about forgetting. There are some things we do forget, but there are also some things we'll never forget.

If we don't let go of our past, then our only option is to continue living in our past, defeated. This results in our frequently reliving our emotional hurts.[13] It is like removing a scab from our skin before it is healed, so our wound never heals; but we are always in the process of being healed. Living in our past can keep us from living completely in our present. Looking backward distracts us from taking advantage of present time with loved ones and life opportunities. Living in our past may create a fear of living in the present. We can unintentionally become a prisoner of our past.

Living in our past will steal our time from family, loved ones, our present, and our future. Have you ever been with family or loved ones, but something is so pressing you that you are physically there, but not there emotionally or mentally? You may be in the room but not even hear conversations.

Our family and loved ones are so valuable that we need to be present with them as much as possible.

Often, I tell people addicted to pornography that I'm counseling that they will have to make *a non-emotional decision to a very emotional temptation.* I tell them that they have to see the "Big Picture" in regard to the cycle of pornography if they are going to defeat their addiction.

The same is true with our letting go of our past. If we are able mentally, we will need to apply this same principle to letting go of our past.

As I've said before, one of my favorite sayings is "Don't let the pain of your past punish your present, paralyze your future, and pervert your purpose because you have a godly destiny."

Here are some benefits of letting go:

- Brings us more intimacy in understanding more clearly Christ's pain of rejection.

- Releases/frees us to move on (GOMO: Get Over Move On) to function more effectively for God in the present, instead of constantly living in the *past*. Remember, the *war* has already been *won* by *God*!

- Allows us to begin the process of understanding the rejection issue. (God told Samuel, his prophet, "They are not rejecting you, but they are rejecting *me, God*" [see 1 Samuel 8:7].)

- Provides us with insight into God's incredible love for us and his patience with us.

- Can also begin the process of emotional detachment. We must be careful here not to allow our emotional detachment to lead us to resentment and bitterness. The detachment is a critical step if God is in the process of releasing us from our prison to emotional freedom.

- Helps us begin understanding that our situation is often bigger than us and not just about us! Let go of the self-pity. So, in letting go, we can't worry about what our situation looks like to anyone other than God. We may look like a failure. Don't try to justify your situation. We must concentrate on what our relationship with God *is*!

- Can lead to the *time of your life!*

- Requires an attitude of trust in God and a mental adjustment to try to see God's big picture. Don't see the people who hurt us as our enemy, but see the spirit behind those people—especially if they are Christians.

- Opens a door to more understanding, more freedom from depression, stress, and competition. It requires dependency on God's sovereignty, resulting in a calming and calmer spirit, also a "Wait and see" spirit/attitude. We gain more peace because we are in our proper and safe place of *following God* instead of trying to lead him. Our desire to control or manipulate the situation lessens because people's inability to recognize what a tremendous gift of God we are becomes less of an issue for us. Remember to understand the difference between self-worship and self-worth.

- Begins God's transforming us into a more effective servant for him, being more in tune with pleasing him. It develops more of a servant spirit in us. "How can we give more?" instead of "What do we get?"

- Provides more patience with families and ourselves because we are not so focused only on ourselves and depressed and obsessed with receiving justice, which can result in a short temper with them. It gives us more security knowing who we are in Christ.

- Releases us to a deeper level of worshiping God. We get a freedom to worship God as never before. God reveals more of himself to us because we are now in a position to trust him as we sit at his feet, now open to learning whatever he wants to teach us, resulting in our wanting to worship him more for *who he is*, not for what he can do for us![14]

God forgives us for his own sake, and he never remembers our sins anymore once they are forgiven; so this means that if or when we have thoughts that remind us of our past sins, mistakes, or whatever, those thoughts are not from God. Therefore, we need to learn how to deal with these negative thoughts.

Second Corinthians 10:5b says, "We capture their rebellious thoughts and teach them to obey Christ." When a negative thought comes to mind, we should ask God for help. I recommend a prayer like this: "Dear God, I know this thought is not from you and is probably from Satan, my enemy. I don't want to focus on this thought. Please take it away from me. I trust you to help me."

The incident of my mistreating John reminded me of three more incidents in which I hurt other people in the area of finances. These were not fond memories to relive. I was able to make restitution. I had to forgive myself for these, too.

But this is so essential to know and embrace: I'm not the same person that I was. *I can't undo the past, but I don't have to let my past undo me!*

Letting go of your past can open the door of freedom to live in your present time and even plan for the future.

WHY YOU NEED TO LIKE YOU: FOR YOURSELF AND THOSE WHO LOVE YOU

I believe it is essential for us to like ourselves. If we don't like ourselves, a tough but fair question is, why should anyone else like us?

Consider this: if we don't like ourselves, subconsciously, we emit negatives vibes or emotions from ourselves about ourselves. This can make us unattractive to other people, even if we are good looking or dressed nicely.

If we don't like ourselves, we may be needy. When we become needy, we can become co-dependent; then, we can unintentionally become selfish and dysfunctional. Dysfunctionality often leads to self-destruction. When we are selfish, we unintentionally put those around us on a performance track to please us. And if they don't please us, we often will become upset with them. This is devastating to relationships.

When we like ourselves, we are easy and fun to be around. When we like ourselves, we make it easier for others to like us. There may be people who would like to be our friends but are uncomfortable with us because we don't seem to like ourselves. When we like ourselves, we demonstrate that we know that God loves us. When we like ourselves, our focus is not only on ourselves, but also on those around us. We can now be sensitive to their possible needs and help them if necessary. So now, by living in the present, we can become a benefit to others.

When we give to others, I believe we always receive more than we give.

What does Dr. Mo have to say about giving yourself grace? Let's answer a few questions after our time on Dr. Mo's couch.

DR. MO'S COUCH

Forgiving ourselves, loving ourselves, liking ourselves, giving ourselves grace—all of these can be so very difficult. And it can be complicated to try to discover the reasons why. It can also be downright frightening to have to face the culprit or culprits that can explain this relationship we have with ourselves.

Clarence has already given examples of how some of our actions and experiences can create this sense of low self-worth and layered guilt that we live with for years. It is indeed a process to acknowledge what is the core reasoning for our thoughts and the healing journey toward undoing the cognitive distortions over time.

One of the most important and freeing distinctions for me to make among my clients is helping them to distinguish between feelings and thoughts. We can choose to forgive ourselves with a single act of the will. We make a choice. It's not always based on what we feel because, if so, we would be like Clarence. We would

Dr. Mo: "How y'all coming along?"

Clarence: "I'm doing okay in a good way."

Dr. Mo: "Praise the Lord!"

Clarence: "More and more I'm seeing benefits of experiencing my dark place and God bringing me out. I'm much more at peace with myself."

Dr. Mo: "Are you adding these additional insights to your depression book?"

Clarence: "Some. I'm trying to finish the leader's guide for my other book. So I am slowly getting things done."

Dr. Mo: "Awesome!! This is exciting!!"

Clarence: "I'm thinking about rereading *I Don't Want To Talk About It*[16] It may inspire me to write another book, but I have three book writing projects ahead of it."

Dr. Mo: "Now, THAT is for real some good exciting news!!"

Clarence: "Can we talk some when you have time?"

Dr. Mo: "Sure."

carry around already-forgiven guilt (at least by God if not by others) for years.

Some experiences are so traumatic in nature, so deeply embedded in our psyche, that it might require time in therapy to process them. We do not have to feel bad about needing therapy. We need to understand the unique and complex intricacies of experiences with trauma to give reassurance and insight to why some of us struggle with forgiveness of self and grace giving. Depending on the nature of some of our life's experiences, it is understandable why we are so hard on ourselves. And why it takes time to believe that God forgives *even me*. Yes, he who died and suffered for *us*! It is indeed hard to believe.

It takes a skilled therapist to begin the process of chipping away at the layers upon layers of numbness, dissociation, guilt, shame, hurt, fear, anger, sadness, depression, stress, and whatever else blocks that truth. Usually we are buried under all of these feelings. If we can understand that God really loves us, and therefore from that truth, we can begin to love ourselves, we can begin the journey toward true healing. God has already won the battle, as Clarence stated. We just have to walk in the truth that his work is fully completed in us. We have to begin the process of working out that which is already in us.

Many of us say we have let things go but still live as though they are not gone. That's because we say that as if it were a magical chant. Poof! Be gone. But more times than not, it isn't. Usually, it will be a process that we have to walk through. God can show us things in our lives that may not feel the best once we see these things for ourselves. But that is a way that God begins showing us what's inside of us that ultimately needs to be healed. He reveals those things that potentially keep us from loving ourselves and forgiving ourselves too.

And what about God's sufficient grace? God promises us that when we are weak, *he* will be made strong. He comes in us and alongside us to assist us with the hard parts of our life's journey. He will show us that we can forgive ourselves. The enormity of his love for us will embrace us to the point that we will *know* and *feel* the love of God. Yes, we still have to wrestle and take those negative thoughts into captivity at times. But the moment we can recognize the love God has for us is the moment I believe our healing can be accelerated. Now we can experience what he wants to give us as opposed to just knowing what we have read and heard.

YOUR JOURNEY

Remember how God sees us? He wants us, so he created us. And because he made us in his image, we have his DNA. We have value, purpose, and a destiny. We need to accept this concept of self-worth. It is okay and healthy to know that we have value.

- From 1–10, rate yourself on how you are at giving grace to yourself. Was your rating high, low, or in the middle? Why do you think that is?

- What do you think others would say about your rating of yourself?

What are some of the ways that you beat yourself up?

1. _____

_____

2. _____

_____

3. _____

_____

- Why do you think you beat yourself up?

- How do you feel after beating yourself up?

- What do you think about the concept of forgiving yourself? If you can forgive yourself, how do you think you will feel about yourself?

- How can the tips about letting go of your past help you if you are having difficulty letting go of your past?

- When will you begin to try letting go of your past, if this is an issue for you?

- How do you feel about the concept that you should like yourself?

- How do you feel about the idea that God wanted you, created you with his DNA, and that you have value, purpose, and a destiny?

CHAPTER ELEVEN

FINDING A GOOD AND EFFECTIVE COUNSELOR

My last bout with depression made it obvious to me that I needed help. I required the help of a professional counselor. I asked God to heal me himself. He provided Dr. Mo. She was and is simply amazing and exactly what I needed!

The format of this book was for me to share my depression experiences, then, Dr. Mo provided her professional expertise and insight with regard to what I was dealing with. She also shared possible tips for you if you struggle with some of the same issues that I did. Honestly, I had some shame connected with this idea of needing a counselor. I counsel people all the time. Why couldn't I just counsel myself? I felt God urged me to get counseling. Thus, I reluctantly asked Dr. Mo if she would counsel me. Initially, I put parameters on her counseling me. She was extremely patient with me, knowing that I needed her help more than I realized. I was trying to control the counseling because I kept thinking I didn't want it.

Maybe you are like me. You know you need counseling, but you feel shame or negative feeling about having a counselor.

For me, having Dr. Mo as a counselor was life-changing! She helped me better understand myself. She also saw things about me that I couldn't see. Maybe most critical for me was that she provided a safe place, a voice of calm in the midst of chaos, and God used her to give me hope!

> "A good counselor creates a *safe place* for you so you can talk about anything because you know it is confidential! You should feel comfortable with your counselor."

After reading this book, you may realize that you need counseling. So Dr. Mo and I want to provide some practical steps in finding an effective counselor if you need one because not all counselors unfortunately are always good counselors.

Primarily, my counseling is in the area of relationships, mostly interpersonal, but some with organizations. I also conduct biblical diversity training. Easily, marriage is the bulk of my counseling, but I also assist singles, families, couples desiring to overcome affairs, and those struggling with pornography. Most recently, I've begun to spend more time with church youth groups and college campuses (separating young men and women) discussing friendships with the opposite sex, dating, biblical sex, pornography, and sexting.

A GOOD WAY TO FIND A COUNSELOR

Often my new clients are referred to me from former clients. And unfortunately, some clients come to me after having a bad experience with another counselor.

Possibly the best way to find a counselor is when one of your friends recommends one to you. You may ask some of your good friends (individually) if any of them ever needed counseling, and if so, whom would they recommend.

Often if a friend recommends a counselor, it is because that counselor helped them or someone they know. If the counselor helped your friend, then, because your friend knows you, he or she knows if the counselor is a good fit for you. This is not a guarantee but a good possibility.

WHAT MAKES A COUNSELOR EFFECTIVE?

A good counselor creates a *safe place* for you so you can talk about anything because you know it is confidential! You should feel comfortable with your counselor. Simultaneously, your counselor may gently challenge you to examine yourself and your motives, which may be uncomfortable for you, but you need to do it.

An effective counselor gives homework and holds you accountable to do it. Receiving homework as a client provides that opportunity for you to heal or grow. It also maximizes your session time with your counselor. Homework aids your counselor in evaluating you, enabling your counselor to often go deeper with you more quickly, resulting in a quicker healing for you, fewer sessions, and less money.

When you have two or three possible counselor candidates, consider asking each of them for an opportunity to interview them as a potential counselor for you. If possible, and it may not be possible due to legal confidentially issues, ask the counselor if there is a former client or two whom you could call or meet, not to discuss their issue, but to ask questions regarding the counselor's style, techniques, and effectiveness.

You may need to meet with a particular counselor one or two times to see if it is a fit or not. It is fine, if after two or three sessions you feel your counselor is not a fit, to seek a new counselor. But please don't discontinue meeting with a counselor because he or she challenges you to examine yourself more than you feel comfortable doing. This is what it may take to help or heal you emotionally.

If you are seeking a Christian counselor, I suggest you pray about this.

For example, if you decide your marriage requires counseling, let me suggest that the two of you pray as a couple for God to lead you to a Christian counselor who will be best for your particular situation. As a couple, try to agree on a counselor so the counselor isn't viewed to be on one spouse's side and against the other. Seek to secure a counselor who will hold both individuals accountable for the marriage.

If your Christian counselor isn't using the Bible as his or her counseling authority and that's what you want, ask if more biblical principles can be examined. If not, then find another counselor. I'm not suggesting the counselor preach a sermon or that every word has to reference the Bible. Yet he or she should be familiar with the biblical relationship principles.

A good counselor will provide options for you in regard to making choices. If the counselor tells you exactly what to do in every instance, your confidence and dependence on your counselor can become unhealthy. But if your counselor helps you to learn to make your own wise decisions (with God's help), then you become emotionally healthier and not co-dependent. You can develop a healthy understanding of self-worth (not self-worship). And you also grow in your faith and intimacy with God.

A good counselor will charge you a reasonable fee. Compare it to going to a physician's office. Typically, if we don't have to pay for help, we tend not to value it. Frequently, our motivation to do what we're asked to do by a medical doctor or counselor is motivated by the fact that we've made a financial investment.

WHEN TO CONSIDER CHANGING COUNSELORS

If a counselor asks you to violate biblical principles, stop the counseling sessions immediately.

If a counselor tells you to separate and live in different places, you may need to seriously consider terminating the counseling sessions with this counselor, unless there is physical abuse. Most of the couples I have known that had marriage problems and were advised by their counselor to separate usually got divorced after separating. Typically, most struggling marriage couples have a much better chance of resolving their problems while they are living together.

Separation and isolation often create an insurmountable emotional distance that eventually destroys the marriage. In such an environment, it is so easy to focus only on yourself, which can unintentionally make an individual more selfish. Marriage is about giving and serving. In isolation, it is often easy to blame your spouse for all the problems in your marriage. And Satan often uses the divide and conquer tactic very successfully with couples.

SOME FINAL THOUGHTS TO CONSIDER

From my perspective, a counselor's goal is to work herself or himself out of a job. For example, you may need to attend counseling sessions weekly for a while, but eventually, as progress is made, the counseling goes to twice a month, then once a month, until you as the client are released. The time between sessions is perfect for homework.

Also, just because a counselor is on a referral list doesn't equate to that particular counselor being a good one. Sometimes counselors may have to pay a fee to be on certain referral lists. So do your homework to find the counselor that will be the most effective for you.

Disclaimer: If you are in counseling and need medication to help you with your depression, the following may not be true for you. Please follow the instructions of your counselor.

There are some well-meaning churches that provide free counseling. Former clients of this free counseling in my area often come to me for help. They have no problem paying for my services because they are being helped and can experience a difference.

Once, I actually lost a client couple because I didn't charge them. They seemed to be having financial difficulty. They fired me. Three months later, they returned and wanted to pay my fee!

I'm sure that there are some tremendous free counselors, but often, you get what you pay for!

DR. MO'S COUCH

Since I'm not licensed to practice in Clarence's home state, I suggested he pursue another counselor. I just wanted him to be okay. I knew he needed to acknowledge his depression and then seek out assistance for dealing with it. I suspected Clarence was depressed after he shared with me about a devastating experience. He and I are regularly in contact, so I was usually aware of most of his activities. I had an idea of the accumulation of disappointments and stressful events he endured. When I heard him share about the latest encounter, I sensed he was depressed. It sounded as though it was the "last straw that broke the camel's back" tone. I'm not saying everyone has to be depressed when they encounter trial after trial and disappointment after disappointment. However, as a trained clinician, I discerned Clarence was depressed.

I asked him some direct questions to determine if my hypothesis might be accurate. I shared with him some professional insights to encourage him to realize depression is real and it could be something he was battling. Most African American men tend to dismiss, minimize, or altogether ignore the fact that they might be depressed. Knowing this fact, I urged Clarence to consider he could be struggling with depression.

At times, individuals feel weak or embarrassed to admit they might be depressed. But we have to understand that in the spaces of life that are tough (*"Many* are the afflictions of the righteous" [Psalm 34:19 KJV, emphasis mine]), depression is a normal emotional response and state. I have observed in my numerous years of clinical work that depression is prolonged due to failure to acknowledge it. It is prolonged because there is no intervention. You cannot seek healing for that which you will not admit or recognize needs healing.

You might be depressed or recognize someone else is depressed. Please consider going along with someone to have an evaluation. Most times when people decide to go for counseling, it is usually not a "fly-by-the-seat-of-your-pants" decision. Some feel it is a last-ditch effort for whatever their issue is. Others have engaged in conversation with friends or family who went to counseling. Then there are some who may agree to go reluctantly.

In counseling, the therapeutic relationship is one of the most determining factors as to the effectiveness of counseling. Therefore, it is important to know what you want in and from a counselor. Some counselors may allow for a ten-to-fifteen-minute phone conversation prior to you scheduling an appointment with them. This may give some indication if you want to meet with that particular counselor or not. If you have no experience with counseling, you may not be sure of what to look for in a counselor. Feeling safe, heard, supported, and valued might be some of the core factors you want a counselor to possess.

Counselors have various orientations and approaches for therapy. It will be good to speak with them or visit their website to obtain a more thorough understanding of their modalities. Again, determine what seems to align with your desires, needs, and beliefs.

Most of my clients seek my services because I explicitly state that I am a Christian counselor. Over time, there has been much controversy between theology and psychology. Some Christians have been opposed to any counseling outside of biblical counseling. There are therapists, such as myself, who have been trained in the integration of psychology and theology. And then there are some who are Christians that are counselors. I would argue there are distinctions or there would be no need for a training program to exist.

There are different categories of mental health clinicians. I will distinguish them for you:

- Psychiatrist: Medical doctors who sometimes provide medication, assess physical conditions, and diagnose medical problems. This is the only mental health professional that can prescribe mediations. Your primary physician may also prescribe medications or refer you to a psychiatrist.

- Psychologist: Many specialties exist. Most deal with abnormal behavior, severe emotional disturbances, psychological testing, and provide psychotherapy.

- Counselor: Focuses on promotion and maintenance of mental health, and prevention and treatment of mental illness—emphasizing wellness.

- Pastoral counselor: Have received training theologically along with some clinical studies.

- Biblical counselor: Typically are lay counselors who solely use the Bible to advise people. Sometimes the term "biblical counselor" is used interchangeably with "Christian counselor." You can inquire about the level of training biblical counselors have received and the level of clinical training obtained. This information will help you in your counselor selection.

Word-of-mouth referrals are sometimes the most effective ways to find a counselor. However, you may be able to ask your medical doctor for a referral too. Some insurance companies will help to pinpoint a counselor with a certain specialty in your geographical location. There are referrals sources such as Psychology Today, American Association of Christian Counselors, or Therapy for Black Girls.

YOUR JOURNEY

A good counselor creates a *safe place* for you so you can talk about anything because you know it is confidential! You should feel comfortable with your counselor. Simultaneously, your counselor may gently challenge you to examine yourself and your motives, which may be uncomfortable for you, but you need to do it!

- What are your initial thoughts about counseling?

- Do you have shame or negative feelings associated with counseling? If so, why?

- What would be your biggest fear about counseling? Why?

Have you had a previous experience that didn't go well? If so, did you tell anyone? Do you feel you received the support you needed?

1. _____

_____

2. _____

_____

3. _____

_____

- There is misinformation about counselors. How were Dr. Mo's insights about counseling helpful?

- Why do you think more and more people seem to think that counseling is a good idea?

CHAPTER TWELVE

WAYS THE CHURCH CAN HELP

Easter Sunday of 2021, Christina, my oldest daughter, invited me to visit her new church. Her senior pastor Craig Groeschel's sermon was "When You Feel Like Giving Up."[16] During his sermon, he revealed that he had emotional issues. He shared that he, the pastor of Life Church, a megachurch, has a counselor. Pastor Groeschel said this counselor has helped him tremendously—specifically, that his counselor helped him to recognize that the strongest unhealthy driver in his life is shame.

What leaders publicly do this? I'm listening to this service thinking, *Wow! More pastors need to do this!*

HOW SOME PASTORS CAN HELP THEIR CHURCHES

Pastor Groeschel began his 2020 Easter sermon by saying, "I'm going to tell you about my breakdown." His sermon title was "When Life Is Out of Control."[17] As I think of this pastor, two thoughts come to mind: (1) I'm so glad that my daughter is going to this church; and (2) this pastor preaches where his people live.

Pastor Groeschel's transparency was and is an incredible gift to the members of Life Church! By publicly sharing with his congregation and anybody with access to YouTube that he had or has emotional issues, he immediately created a *safe place* for church members under his leadership. He has given them permission not to be "fine" and not to have to fake it when they are struggling emotionally.

The fact that Pastor Groeschel publicized that he has a counselor communicated that it is okay to get professional emotional and mental help. Seeking such help doesn't make you any more abnormal than anyone else.

Imagine how the emotionally wounded people who heard this message may have immediately been set free to seek help without the stigma of shame.

So how can the church help? Maybe the first, easiest, and possibly the most effective way would be if more pastors who have had or have emotional issues would courageously be more transparent. *Stop!* I'm not recommending that pastors tell publicly their biggest and darkest secrets. All pastors who are considering becoming more transparent should pray about any sharing that would put them in a position of vulnerability. If you are such a pastor, you should:

- Consider asking your spouse for input that would be invaluable.

- Refrain from sharing anything about your spouse that would embarrass them or blindside them. Unfortunately, I've embarrassed my wife. Don't do it!

- If your spouse gives you permission and affirms you in being transparent, then pray before speaking to the church's leadership.

- If your leadership gives you the "okay," then bathe this decision in prayer before publicly sharing with the congregation. And please don't feel you have to do this every Sunday.

- Be who God created you to be. You don't need to cry during every sermon in order to attempt to prove that you are sensitive. But preaching two to four times a year about emotions or depression could be a tremendous blessing for those listening to you weekly. You don't have do all the sharing. You could have members who feel comfortable sharing two to five minutes of their emotional struggles. Their sharing, with the advice of a licensed counselor prepping them before they publicly speak, could be just as powerful after the pastor has shared first.

Another way the church could possibly help members when they are in a dark place or before they get there would be to preach and teach about depression. David's writing in the Bible in Psalm 32:3–8 is an excellent text for teaching about depression. There are defined symptoms of depression. In this case (but not all cases), David was the source for his own depression. Please don't say that all depression is because of sin or not being spiritual enough.

Jeremiah 20:7–18 is another excellent biblical text dealing with depression due to disappointment in being frustrated with God.

A two-to-three-week series of preaching about depression could significantly bless church members. One of those Sundays, you could interview a licensed counselor during the service instead of preaching—the world won't end! It would be wise to secure the insight of a counselor like Dr. Mo for wisdom in regard to what to be aware of, and do's and don'ts.

HEALTHY CHURCHES REQUIRE
HEALTHY PASTORS

Having worked with hundreds of pastors and continuing to work with them, I know that it is absolutely essential that pastors have an accountability system in place. Pastors without accountability systems tend to fall morally. And it is common for pastors with absolute authority to poorly manage churches.

I found it was invaluable having a board of elders to whom I was accountable. Matthew 8:9 reads, "I know this because I am under the authority of my superior officers, and I have authority over my soldiers." The biblical principle of appropriately using authority—that an individual needs to be under authority—works!

Our elder board was extremely close as some of us were friends before I started the church. We ate together, played basketball together (extremely competitive), and respected each other! We love the Lord and each other. We spoke frankly in our elder meeting and could strongly disagree; then we'd go eat. We learned to submit to each other. And even though I started the church, had more years in ministry, and had more formal biblical education, I submitted to the elders' leadership.

One elder told me once when a woman in our church other than my wife was interested in me. He protected me because I had no idea.

When pastors don't have this kind of accountability in place, they can fall morally.

When pastors don't have this kind of accountability, they can be seduced by power.

Churches where the pastor has complete control, and also those where the pastor has 51 percent leadership, can result in the same thing. When leading just by what they think and feel, these pastors can poorly manage the church. Instead, securing additional input would be better for the church. The saying "Absolute power corrupts absolutely" is true.

This accountability can help pastors with their marriages and even depression if the pastor has leadership (elder or deacon board, etc.) that is respected and listened to.

Pastors don't like to be hypocrites, so if they are struggling with their marriages, most are not going to preach about marriage. If they are struggling with depression, most aren't going to preach about this either.

One of the best things a pastor can do for his family, church, and himself is to have a healthy accountability system in place. A healthy church requires a healthy pastor.

CONSIDER FAMILY ADOPTION

My former pastor, the late Dr. Mark Corts, challenged his congregation to adopt college students, especially those away from home, as part of their families. Students loved this, and the families were usually blessed as well. Or what if your pastor encouraged the members of the church not only to adopt college students, but singles of any age? Don't limit this to college students. Just having a church family that is imperfect like everything else could become a safe place for an individual who feels alone and hopeless.

CONSIDER HIRING A COUNSELOR
AS CHURCH STAFF.

A third possible way of assisting churches to aid its members would be to hire a counselor for the staff and church. Dr. Mo has served a church in this capacity, so we'll get her insight later. Another friend of mine serves his fifteen-thousand-plus member church as its counselor. Naturally, he can't counsel the entire church himself, so he has certified a staff of lay counselors for the church.

SOME CHURCH CULTURES CAN
HELP THEIR MEMBERS

Surprisingly, my initial thoughts of how the church can help took me back to my childhood.

When I was envisioning how our churches can help us, its members, when we are battling depression, the traditional Black church immediately came to my mind. Certainly, no one church, denomination, or culture has the market cornered successfully regarding handling depression corporately. But perhaps churches of color, possibly the African, African American, and Hispanic/Latino churches, can help other churches and cultures address the issue of depression in a corporate setting. Or other expressive church cultures may be able to assist.

The primary characterization of the traditional Black church is that it is full of emotional expression!

Something that I've never forgotten is that, during segregation, when I was a nine- or ten-year-old, during our church service, a man was shouting. His shouting seemed uncontrollable and endless. Yet no one ushered him out of the church or seemed to be upset by his loud and continuous shouts, even after most of the shouting had ceased.

After that church service, as we walked to the car with Dad and Jean, my sister, I asked, "Mom, why did that man shout so long?" She smiled and replied, "Honey, I don't think that man knows Jesus. But he comes to church every now and then, especially when he's had a hard week. His shouting is his way of releasing all the emotional hurt from rejections and other difficult situations that he faced during the past week. The shouting frees him up so he can face tomorrow."

"Imagine belonging to a church in which it is okay to cry."

Mom's words were so profound that I never forgot them. Today, as a man, a Black man in particular, with so many systems that seem to oppose men of color, especially the shooting of unarmed African Americans, I totally understand why that man needed to shout and how it possibly kept him sane.

Imagine belonging to a church in which it is okay to cry as a man or a woman. Imagine belonging to such a church that if you need a hug, need to kneel on the steps of the pulpit to pray or just moan, no one thinks that you are crazy! Few if anyone in such a church would think you are irrational because most Blacks and other people of color—men, women, boys, and girls—have experienced some kind of injustice. So, in most (not all) Black churches, the majority of attendees have a fairly accurate assessment of what an individual is experiencing when he or she cries or shouts in church. Thus, there is little judgment for emotional outbursts. It is a safe place for most people.

Often the music of a Black choir sets the tone for a particular Sunday service. Sometimes the music is all an individual needs in order to release his or her emotional baggage.

The truth be told, these emotional outbursts can be incredibly therapeutic, whether they are a response to life in general as a person of color or as a woman, to worship music, or to a sermon!

More and more contemporary churches that tend to be more diverse than traditional or mainline churches are freer in their worship services, with an emphasis on raising hands and movement. Some of these worship services may last for twenty-five minutes or longer, similar to traditional Black churches.

There is something about corporate worship that allows individuals to feel safe enough and to feel the freedom to express their emotions. Their expressions are without thoughts of shame or rejection.

WHAT ABOUT THE WHITE
CHURCH AND EMOTION?

Members of one primarily White denomination calls themselves "the frozen chosen"; but they are not the only primarily White denomination that seem to feel that emotion is inappropriate. But Whites do have emotion. Just attend a sporting event and watch them support their team. You will see plenty of emotion.

Dr. Martin Davidson, the Johnson and Higgins Professor of Business Administration at the University of Virginia's Darden Graduate School of Business, revealed in his research regarding conflict between African Americans and Caucasians in the work-place that Caucasians generally view the expressing of emotions as a lack of intelligence, typically believing that people who express emotions are usually out of control.[18]

If expressing your emotions is viewed as exhibiting a lack of intelligence in your culture, what do you do with your emotions? Emotions are often legitimate, appropriate, healthy, and natural. Emotions can be manipulated. Often, when speaking to young men, I say, "Boys are controlled by their emotions, but men control their emotions. Men don't deny their emotions, but they aren't controlled by them."

So corporately, are Whites suppressing their emotions in church? If so, how can their church corporately help?

Before I answer this question, there is at least one more thought for consideration in a predominantly White church. If, in general, this culture as a majority is not accustomed to suffering on a long-term basis or suffering at all, then this idea of things not being fine could be a problem.

Another aspect that could make it difficult for White American conservative Christians to deal with emotion corporately in their churches is their idea that they have to win. So, possibly, if you are White and things aren't perfect or even good, you may feel like a failure. This is not true!

This idea of winning can be seen in several ways. One is by comparing the hymnals in a Caucasian church with the one found in most traditional Black churches. In many White churches, the hymnals usually have more songs about victory. In many of the Black churches, there are more songs about suffering.

Even with book titles, for White publishing companies, winning seems to be a priority. With my first book, I wanted my title to ask the question, "Is Racial Reconciliation Really Working?" The publisher changed it to *Winning the Race to Unity: Is Racial Reconciliation Really Working?* The priority of winning emerges.

So, a mindset of winning and suppressing emotion may make it more difficult for Caucasians even in the context of the church to admit that something is wrong and that help is needed. This in itself is a major problem and an obstacle to overcome before even attempting to work through depression without feeling abnormal or shame.

Caucasian churches more than others may need to be more intentional in addressing depression.

And this is why Pastor Craig Groeschel's sermons are so amazing, timely, and necessary!

GROUPS THAT NEED
THE CHURCH'S HELP NOW

SHOW SINGLES SOME LOVE

When I think of a group in the church that in general struggles going to their church even though they love it, the singles in those churches come to mind. It doesn't matter if these singles have never been married or are divorcees. Usually singles in churches consist of two groups. One group wants to get married yesterday. The other group members are fine being single, not looking to get married, and don't want to be lumped into the group that is looking to get married.

If you ask singles about their churches, most will tell you that they love their church and their pastor. They will tell you that they love belonging.

But almost in the same breath, both groups of singles will also tell you that they feel like second-class church members.

Many singles feel there is a double standard in the church. For example, if a married couple is experiencing difficulty in their marriage, they are often directed to counseling or given some resource. Singles often tell me that if they express to church leadership that they are experiencing a problem, especially if they are struggling with being single, their church leadership usually tells them to "suck it up" spiritually.

Some singles feel that being single keeps them from some church leadership positions.

What should the church do?

Singles would love to have an interactive session with their church leadership. Some churches believe that a single person should not be in leadership. Can you imagine the New Testament without Paul's influence?

A wise pastor will preach about singles in the Bible and how God used them. A wise pastor will listen to singles in order to inform married church members how singles feel and how to serve the singles in their church.

WHY CHURCH IS NOT A SAFE PLACE FOR MOST MEN

In 2005, David Murrow wrote the first edition of his book *Why Men Hate Going to Church*. Instantly, it became a bestseller. David provided incredible yet simple insights as to why many men hate going to church. I haven't read David's book in its entirety. But after I read the introduction and a portion of the first chapter, it is now a must-read for me.

The first fact that David addressed is that the American church has been designed to cater more to women, not men. Since there are usually more women than men in the church, the church culture is feminine. This doesn't appeal to men. The rapid growth of Promise Keepers in the mid-'90s is a confirmation of this. David's research revealed that 61 percent of people in church were women. Pew Research in 2022 shows that 31 percent of men are attending church once a week.[19]

This is not about blaming women. It is about why the church can be a depressing and not safe place for a man. When is the last time you heard a sermon on biblical manhood or how to be a spiritual leader for your wife and family?

One of the first problems is that most pastors are males. Now, don't freak out on me. Hear me out. I'm not making a theological position for or against women pastors. I'm just addressing the reality of what is.

What I am saying is that many male pastors often put men down in church during their sermons. While the pastor's motive may be humility, and he may have the best intentions, every time he puts himself down, he's putting down every man in church.

Sheila Wray Gregoire, author of *Honey, I Don't Have a Headache Tonight: Help for Women Who Want to Feel More "In the Mood,"* said, "I've often noticed that sermons on Mother's Day tend to gush over moms, while on Father's Day they tell dads to 'shape up.'" She goes on to say, "The modern church pushes men out of the pews by ignoring their needs and devaluing their strengths."[20]

Sheila gets it! Our culture portrays men as lazy, stupid, passive, and definitely not the leader of their families. Unfortunately for men of faith, the church preaches a similar message.

The Western church has a double-standard—one for women and one for men. Women are often encouraged, praised, and loved. Men are constantly told what they *are not doing well* but seldom if ever affirmed or praised for what they do well.

When is the last time you heard your pastor esteem or affirm men in church? If you haven't, then neither have the children, nor have their mothers.

I'm so grateful for the pastors that preach about marriage because, in our Western Christian society, you can attend a church and not hear a sermon about marriage for years. And when you do, often the pastor tells the man what he is not doing right. But seldom does the pastor preach about how the man can be that spiritual servant leader that he is being chastised for not being. Many husbands want to be godly husbands and servant leaders. But their pastors are not telling them *how* to develop those skills. Too many pastors just condemn them for not doing what they don't know how to do.

There have been a couple of times in my life that, if I weren't married and had no children, I would have stopped going to church for a while. One of the practices of a pastor at a particular church was that near the end of each of his sermons, he would cry. He seemed disingenuous. He made me crazy! I went to church because there was no way Brenda was going to let me stay home. I began to tune our pastor out and read my Bible during his sermons. We eventually left that church.

It is harder to be a man today than ever before!

Are all churches like this? No!

Dr. Willie Richardson, founder and former senior pastor of Stronghold Christian Church in Philadelphia, created a special men's day in which he celebrated men in his church and community. Being a Christ follower was not a prerequisite for receiving an award for doing something to improve the local community. Pastor Richardson often has seen non-Christ followers who receive this prestigious award begin to attend his church, and many become Christ followers. This award is the Cornelius Award.[21]

By Pastor Richardson's honoring men, wives, mothers, and children learn to honor and respect men. The men in this church feel respected and cared for by their pastor. He can then criticize them, but they know it is because he loves them.

Bishop Courtney McBath has similar events to honor the men in his church, Calvary Revival Church in Norfolk, Virginia. When I met Bishop McBath in 1995, his church had three thousand members. He said that 51 percent of his attendees were men! He was extremely creative and very aware of men. Today, his church is three to four times that size.[22]

What some pastors don't realize is that *respect is like oxygen for men*! When pastors don't respect men from the pulpit, they make it difficult for every man in the pew to breathe. And these men eventually lose respect for their pastor.

When I pastored in Tulsa, Oklahoma, I learned that strong men attracted strong men and strong women. This becomes a win-win for any church.

One of my friends, Vince, helped a church financially by helping the men. Vince encouraged the senior pastor to realize that even though the church had a men's pastor, in reality the senior pastor was the men's ministry guy. The senior pastor changed his approach to the men. The men responded by blessing the church financially.

YOUTH IN YOUR CHURCH NEED AFFECTION & ATTENTION NOW

LifeWay's new research survey revealed that young adults between the ages of eighteen and twenty-two are dropping out of church according to Holly Meyer's January 15, 2019, article in *The Tennessean*. This is approximately two-thirds of eighteen-to-twenty-two-year-olds.[23]

What does this mean? Scott McConnell, executive director of LifeWay Research, said, "That means the church had a chance to share its message and the value of attending with this group, but it didn't stick."

But why didn't the message of their particular church stick? Chris Brooks, pastor of Kairos congregation at Brentwood Baptist Church in Brentwood, Tennessee, says that the majority of those attending Kairos's Tuesday night service are between the ages of twenty-two and twenty-nine. He said, "For whatever reason [those leaving the church] decided that the church is no longer integral to building their faith or their faith is no longer integral to them." Pastor Brooks went on to state that he loves young adults, but that they are selfish and trying to figure out who they are and what they want to do.[24]

As I am someone who interacts with teenagers and college students, the students themselves have told me that they do struggle with being selfish.

According to Meyer's article, the LifeWay survey discovered:

- Nearly all—96 percent—cited life changes, including moving to college and work responsibilities that prevented them from attending.

- Seventy-three percent said church or pastor-related reasons led them to leave. Of those, 32 percent said church members seemed judgmental or hypocritical and 29 percent said that they did not feel connected to others who attended.

- Seventy-three percent named religious, ethical, or political beliefs for dropping out. Of those, 25 percent said they disagreed with the church's stance on political or social issues while 22 percent said they were only attending to please someone else [probably parents].

- And, 63 percent said student and youth ministry reasons contributed to their decision not to go. Of those, 23 percent said they never connected with students in student ministry and 20 percent said the students seemed judgmental or hypocritical.[25]

Based on the survey results, McConnell said, "Wow, we need to help these young people plan ahead."

Based on the second and third bullets above, I'm certainly not against discussing the future with young people. But the priority seems to be more that leadership in church needs to focus on listening to young people more than attempting to plan their future.

When I ask young people (high school and college age) why they like to interact with me, they list two reasons: (1) "You are transparent" and (2) "You are authentic." Being authentic doesn't require having all the answers. It includes saying, "I don't know. Let me find out." Also, young people love that I ask their permission to begin a discussion with them and that I ask for their opinion. It demonstrates respect, which many feel they don't receive in their churches.

After I had an interactive session about pornography and sexuality with White teenage girls in their church (with five mothers in attendance), the teenage girl who had asked her father to have me speak with the girls said this to me: "Thanks for telling it to us straight. Nobody in our church would have done this."

After one of my "Women's Only" sessions on a Christian college campus, a female student said, "Thank you so much for talking with us and letting us ask questions. People think we as Christian young ladies are pure and don't have sexual temptations. It was great being able to discuss lust and masturbation in a safe place."

One reason our young people stop attending church is because church as they know it is becoming more and more irrelevant to them because it doesn't speak to the issues with which they are struggling.

This is a major issue in traditional conservative churches. When President Obama ran for president the first time, Whites ages eighteen through thirty-nine overwhelmingly voted for him. But most of their parents did not.

Recent social justice issues find that White conservative churches often share their political views from the pulpit as there seems to be a blending of politics and the gospel. Young White people tend to have a different Christian/political view than their parents and the leadership of these churches.[26]

Please don't miss the point here: it is not about politics or your political party of preference. But it is all about listening to the young people and young adults in your church. It is critical for them to feel that church is a safe place for them to disagree.

They view the majority of church leadership as being judgmental or hypocritical.

The church can't continue to approach uncomfortable subjects as the tennis directors of the four Grand Slams did with Naomi Osaka in June of 2021.

At the 2021 French Tennis Open, Naomi Osaka stated before the tournament began that she would not attend the required press conference after each match. After winning her first-round match, she didn't attend the press conference and was immediately fined $15,000 by the French Open Tournament organization and, technically, the Roland-Garros referee. The tennis directors of each of the Grand Slam tournaments threw down the gauntlet by promising even more severe fines and possible expulsion. Osaka responded by withdrawing from the tournament.

Unfortunately, the tennis governing bodies were clueless as to how a person trying to cope with depression might respond. Their bully approach caused Osaka to retreat with the support of many of her tennis peers and celebrities. She said that she didn't want to be the center of attention at the tournament and cause problems for others.

Osaka's emotions and the emotions of the tennis governing bodies were on full display. She later withdrew from several future tournaments, including Wimbledon that year.

Often, when I am counseling a couple whose relationship is struggling, once we have a trusted relationship, I'll say, "One of you has to be the adult."

If the governing tennis bodies would have gone to Osaka instead of expecting a wounded individual to come to them, possibly something could have been resolved privately. But when all you know is showing force, there will be casualties.

To be fair to the tennis governing bodies, someone on Osaka's team should have communicated with the governing bodies as soon as they knew about Osaka's concerns.

> "Now the more visible racial tension for some in America is another issue that the church must address biblically and not politically."

CHURCH LEADERSHIP MUST RECOGNIZE THEIR WALKING WOUNDED

There are groups in our churches that are emotionally wounded and have been for some time, even before we faced COVID-19. Now the more visible racial tension for some in America is another issue that the church must address biblically and not politically.

"No one ever talks about depression in church!" and "Your sermon helped me realize that I'm not crazy!" were the most common responses I received after I began preaching about my depression, first at the Fatherhood CoMission Summit and then at several churches. These responses were and are a cry for help directed toward the church leadership. Our pastors must address these issues where people are hurting. As a former pastor, I'm not trying to beat pastors up. You need love and help too.

OUR EMOTION MUST
BE BASED ON FACT

As critical as it is to get our emotions recognized and on the table, we also need faith that is based on fact.

When I refer to faith based on fact, this is not to imply that if you have enough faith, you'll never struggle with depression. It means that we all need something to believe in as a compass. Looking to this compass provides direction toward a safe place. I believe this compass must be the word of God.

Let's hear what Dr. Mo has to say about how the church can help its members process emotion.

DR. MO'S COUCH

Oh, the numerous ways I've imagined and enacted helping churches to consider their members that will be adversely impacted emotionally and mentally and, yes, even spiritually by dark places. We must prepare the overall environment, specific, and designated spaces for those who are in dark places.

As a former church counselor, I frequently thought of ways the church could serve not only the individuals who came into my office, but also assess the health of the system that is called the church, the local body of Christ.

Imagine if you have a family member who has experienced a broken leg. Maybe the leg is broken in three different places. You immediately start thinking of places in the house where you can rearrange furniture, set up a bed, and provide easy accessibility to the bathroom. You are thinking not only of your family member, but also the environment in which he or she will have to navigate.

And, to some degree, this is how the church should think, not only as individuals but also of the body as a whole. Now, no one church can address every detail as it relates to each specific person. However, there are some general steps that can be implemented to communicate that your church cares for those who are struggling in those dark places.

I agree with Clarence that pastors can help! In those church settings where pastors are influential in decisions being made, they should most definitely utilize the platform, or the pulpit, to help those in dark places.

As Clarence stated, hearing a message preached from the pulpit on depression or other mental and emotional concerns sends a tone throughout the church environment that normalizes the struggles of people. People can feel freer to discuss these tough times in Sunday school classes, small groups, or topic-specific groups because it's natural and comfortable to do so. Because the environment has been arranged or rearranged to allow for the navigation of difficult topics.

The authenticity of leaders can also signal to the members that this church does not shy away from the tough experiences of life. Again, leaders can normalize tough times by saying there has been a tough season and this is what we have learned or gained by going to counseling, sitting with mentors, joining a support group, or taking time away. Naming effective strategies opens up possibilities for members to consider things maybe they would not otherwise.

Along with speaking about these matters from the pulpit, pastors can lead the way in again establishing the environment with ministries and groups and programs that promote mental and emotional well-being.

I have promoted the idea of having groups based on shared experiences. This suggestion can help members with specific lived experiences to recognize they are not alone. There are others who have been through or are going through those same issues. I know it is hard for people to participate in certain groups if they are for survivors of sexual abuse, newly divorced, single parents, overcoming addiction, dealing with anxiety, grief support, and the list goes on and on.

The stigma alone is enough to keep people from participating. The horror of being seen going or coming from the room or area where the food addiction support group is meeting is embarrassing enough to override a person attending the group. I understand the need to dress up the names of the groups to make them more marketable and appealing for people to participate. However, my belief is that we have to call a thing by its name to treat it.

I believe one of the ways that happens is to continue to speak the language associated with mental and emotional distresses. If you name it, express it, and externalize it, then it has no more dominion over you. There is nothing to hide. It is the first step toward liberation. And should this not be how the church should lead others? Toward liberation? First and foremost, liberation over sin. As you ask Jesus to be your Lord, you bring the issues of your lives under his authority. And the more you move toward Jesus, the more you are moving toward liberation.

But if the church does not show up and extend practical guidance in this area, how will others know there is freedom found in Christ to overcome and to deal with the afflictions of this world?

I was hired by a church and served almost seventeen years. It was a fairly large congregation. The church had a few support groups established. I trained the facilitators of those groups. I did not need additional help because it took a while for people to embrace the idea of counseling, even within their own church. Sometimes that was the hinderance—that I was a member of the church as well—and I did my best to keep a low profile to help others feel comfortable when they saw me behind closed doors. I tried to visit the various ministries during their meeting times to eradicate the stigma of mental health services. I wanted to disseminate information that was educational to help equip the members and promote healthy mental and emotional well-being.

Clarence talks about small groups in the next chapter, so some of my comments can be applied to small groups as well.

Here are some suggestions I have for churches if they hire a professional counselor as part of the staff. Counselors are trained to do much more than therapy. For example, I am trained as a mental health clinician and a marriage and family therapist, which means I have expertise in systems. This highlights why I think in terms of the church environment *and* the overall benefit of the individual members that seek out individual counseling. Here are a few suggestions that clinicians could implement if on staff or hired as a consultant:

- Train group leaders. Small groups. Support groups. Discipleship groups. Specific groups (men, women, youth, seniors, etc.). Clarence will talk more extensively about the importance of the group leader. It is crucial that group leaders are *trained* in areas such as group dynamics, basic listening skills, helping skills such as empathy, how to determine if a person is in crisis, what to do if a crisis arises in the group, and how and what to document in groups. These are just a few examples. Insurance companies of churches are increasingly mandating that lay group leaders are trained and that there is a documentation process in place.

- Discuss data during trainings, such as Clarence elaborated on, concerning youth, men, singles, and elderly. This information can be used to strategically plan for these specific populations to ensure better outcomes.

- Write policy and establish procedures to reduce the risk of having groups with inadequate leadership. This can put the church at legal risk. If you do not have a policy on what to do if someone is suicidal in a group (just one example: what do you do when they show up under the influence of some substance?), your church is at great risk if those situations are not handled properly.

- Manage the groups by providing supervision and ongoing training for group leaders. This again is a way to reduce risk when churches show they are actively and continually providing training for group leaders.

- Conduct needs assessments to help churches plan more effectively for ministry outreach.

- Sit in on staff meetings to help evaluate the health and effectiveness of the system (the body) at large. If individual members are discussing inappropriate comments of leaders, lay or hired, then there needs to be an assessment of what's happening in the body. If there are no protocols in place that can be communicated to the church body on how to submit concerns, this may inadvertently send a signal that a member has no recourse in the event there is an occurrence that needs to be reported.

- Provide ongoing support for the real issues that are faced by individuals daily—whether that is racial trauma support or support for receiving a difficult diagnosis. Also, crisis counseling must be available and ready to issue a statement when societal upheavals take place. The church should be ready to give a relevant statement speaking to the emotional and mental effects of cultural and societal traumas. This can include racial or political unrest or even natural disasters. Or the practical and real information that teens and young adults are seeking.

- Educate the body as a whole about healthy emotional expression. And model how that looks within a church environment.

- And lastly, to Clarence's point of family adoption, provide information on healthy family functioning. Everyone does not come from healthy family backgrounds and may not know how to create it or function in it if invited. I do believe family adoption is a *powerful* way to be the family of God we say we are. I believe there is opportunity to do much needed cross-generational connections as well as to educate on the healing nature of corrective emotional experiences and healthy relationships.

So, as you can tell, I am so very passionate about the many ways a Christ-centered, biblically-informed, trained professional can aid the body of Christ. There is no limit to the numerous ways the church can help promote emotional and mental health. However, we do have to be careful to believe it automatically happens just because it is the church. The church must be intentional and strategic in bringing the right leadership in to cultivate the environment and equip the members.

YOUR JOURNEY

Imagine belonging to a church in which it is okay to cry as a man or a woman. Imagine belonging to such a church that if you need a hug, need to kneel on the steps of the pulpit to pray or just moan, no one thinks that you are crazy! Can you?

- How does your church help you process emotional issues corporately?

- If you feel that your church doesn't help you process your emotional issues, why do you think that is?

- If your church doesn't help you process emotional issues, what do you think it could do?

If you are a pastor, how do you think your church corporately helps the members to process their emotions?

1. _____

   _____

2. _____

   _____

3. _____

   _____

If you are a pastor and don't think your church corporately helps the members to process emotions, what would you like to change to help the members corporately?

1. _____

   _____

2. _____

   _____

3. _____

   _____

- How does your church help singles to feel like equal members?

- How does your church make itself safe for men?

- Do the young people feel your church is relevant to them? How do you know this?

CHAPTER THIRTEEN

WAYS YOUR COMMUNITY CAN HELP

S ome of you may be thinking, *But I don't have a community to help me when I'm struggling emotionally.* I hear you! At the end of this chapter, I will share some ideas that you may find helpful, and Dr. Mo will share her insights.

THE SMALL GROUP COMMUNITY

In the last chapter, the question was how the church could help its members with regard to depression. Many churches already have a community of small groups. And some churches have Sunday school in lieu of small groups.

Creating a community of small groups is one action that churches can take to help members.

Churches have options here. Small groups created specifically for those battling depression could be birthed. These specific groups could thrive with a professional counselor or with a group leader trained or certified by a professional counselor. In fact, such groups should require a licensed counselor. But be aware that there could be a stigma attached to such groups.

The other option that I would prefer, and which may be more appealing, would be to have small groups with no specific topic. The leaders in all of the church's small groups could possibly be asked to learn about depression—not to be a counselor, but to be aware of it, and to be a source of help to a group member by being able to privately refer that person to a professional.

> "A skilled small group leader is so essential in order to more effectively serve members of a small group."

A non-specific small group based on a shared interest or geographical neighborhood could be perfect for group members battling depression. The group should be a safe place that has intimacy within the group.

The critical component is the group leader, whether male or female, single or married. Therefore, churches should put time and effort into training their small group leaders.

A skilled small group leader is so essential in order to more effectively serve members of a small group. In a small group, there is almost always an individual who feels they need to prove their knowledge, or seeks to gain affirmation from the group to compensate for insecurity, or attempt to impress everyone. Unfortunately, some individuals try to prove to the group that they should be the group leader. There may be an individual who is extremely quiet. A skilled small group leader knows how to handle all of these variables as well as to graciously encourage the over-talkative person to speak less without offending that individual. They also know how to create an environment so that the super quiet person eventually feels safe to speak. Usually, when a quiet person speaks, what that person says will be so profound for the group and definitely worth the wait!

An experienced and skilled group leader will call each member of the group weekly in order to thank them, to encourage them, to continue to develop the group's intimacy, and to evaluate the group.

Then, a small group can be a safe and intimate place for members to support each other.

THE FAMILY COMMUNITY

We can have all kinds of communities. Of course, my favorite one as a little boy through my junior year of college was my family. Mom was always there for me. I could tell her anything. She literally was always encouraging me. Jean, my older sister, was another confidante. We talked about everything, especially things I didn't want to talk to Dad or Mom about. We were and still are extremely close.

Dad was also my hero. We didn't talk much before I became a Christ follower because Mom said we were so much alike. I didn't see it. I'm not sure Dad did either. Another reason we didn't talk much was he seemed to be working most of the time to financially support us. I had an aversion to hard work. I was also pursuing my god at the time, basketball. Dad was a quiet and serious guy. I loved trying to make him laugh, and I wanted his approval more than anyone else's.

After Dad and I both became Christ followers, our relationship dramatically changed! We talked and listened to each other more. We spent more time together. As I stated earlier, the last time we were together before he died, we prayed together. And before he died, he wrote me a letter my freshman year in college. It was only a few sentences. He only wrote to me once. After his death, I found that letter. Dad wrote, "I saw a young preacher today. He reminded me of you. Keep the faith." He didn't say he loved me. I believe that was about as close to saying he loved me as he could get. But I knew he loved me. I read this letter so often, it finally fell apart in my hands. Dad modeled to me how to be a man, a husband, and a father. He was my anchor.

After Dad died, I felt my role was now to be the head of our family. Thus, I tried to take care of Mom and Jean. I couldn't support them financially like Dad had done. But I could make sure that I was not an emotional burden on them. So I stopped sharing my emotional stressors with them as one of my ways of not burdening and of protecting them. This way, from my perspective, they didn't have to worry about me. But it left me feeling alone. I really needed them more than ever emotionally, I just didn't know it.

Back at college, I didn't have anyone with whom to talk to after Dad's death. Had I had a community of people I trusted, maybe I wouldn't have forgotten my exam schedule and flunked out of school, eventually becoming homeless for a brief period of time.

But my community of family gave me an inner strength to still hope for the best. This was and is a priceless gift from the community of my family.

THE MARRIAGE COMMUNITY

If you're married, your relationship with your spouse can be an incredible support system. Some of you are saying, "I don't have a perfect marriage"—nobody does! And even if your marriage isn't great, the practice of being there for your spouse could possibly transform your marriage into what you've always wanted.

What if your marriage isn't safe for you?

If both of you are Christ followers, whether you feel the marriage is emotionally safe or not, consider praying together with your spouse. Don't think about praying together for an hour or two. Think in terms of two to three minutes. How do you get started? Begin with thanking God for who he is. Then, if you have children, pray for them, pray for your in-laws (your spouse may go into shock—so place a pillow behind them!), pray for your spouse—his or her job, how he or she is feeling emotionally—and pray for your marriage.

Amazingly, research revealed that the key to a happy marriage is praying together. In fact, the research states that the most important and essential thing you can do for your marriage is praying together.

Dr. Phil's book *Relationship Rescue* says that couples who pray together regularly lower their chance of divorce to one out of ten thousand couples!

Think about this! And praying together is *free*!

Praying together builds intimacy.

Also, as a couple, you can read the Bible together in the mornings or before going to bed. Read a chapter or half a chapter together aloud alternating verses, then hold hands and pray. Your spouse and you create a spiritual intimacy. There are also many marriage devotional resources available.

I've had numerous couples read the Bible together aloud and pray at the conclusion. It took them ten to fifteen minutes to do so. Couples said that this practice revolutionized their marriages! Wives said that praying and holding their husbands' hands gave them security. Husbands said hearing their wives pray and holding their hands was encouraging and powerful. One couple in which both had had affairs recommitted their lives and marriage to Christ. Now both are in ministry at their church, and they are helping other marriages. God can do the impossible!

Prayer impacts everything you do as a couple: It will improve your communication—you'll experience more patience. It will lower your conflicts. It will improve your sex life because your sexual relationship is about communication.

Thus, your spouse could drastically impact your depression positively.

THE NEIGHBORHOOD COMMUNITY

Growing up in my neighborhood was so cool! There was a sense of unity and oneness in this community. Adults always encouraged you to do well in everything. It seemed like all the parents knew each other. Families shared food and other resources with each other. And unfortunately for me at the time, any parent in this community could spank you if they saw you misbehaving. I was in trouble daily.

But all of this provided security for me and the other children in my neighborhood.

The phrase "It takes a village to raise a child" unfortunately has been hijacked and made into a political powder keg. But our neighborhood was a village that raised children.

I think those days might be gone forever, or are they?

I've made a special effort to meet my neighbors on my street. They seem to love having someone take the initiative to simply say, "Hello, I'm Clarence, your neighbor, and I live at this address." This usually doesn't result in our becoming best friends. But they do at least become acquaintances who, when we see each other, will often wave or say "Hello." And from time to time, we will help each other. This creates security, peace, and goodwill. Some neighbors have become good friends.

Someone said that our homes today have become our sanctuaries to escape the world. What if we made our home a sanctuary for others in our neighborhoods? It could begin as simply as our taking the first step to show ourselves friendly. Proverbs 18:24 in the New King James Version reads, "A man who has friends must himself be friendly."

Be sure to welcome new neighbors to your community. Take something inexpensive to give as a housewarming gift. This is a great and safe excuse to meet them and open the door to a possible relationship.

COMMUNITY OF
SERVING OTHERS

While I was homeless, a Christian youth center hired me to help with its five hundred African American youth that attended weekly. They became my new community.

I coached the boys and girls basketball teams and ran the Awana games. Awana is a discipleship program for those in preschool to high school. It has its own unique games.

Discipling the young guys on the basketball teams that I coached helped me immensely. These young guys began to help me become less selfish. Definitely not completely selfless—just ask my wife. I still have a photo album of the young men and women at that center, and to this day, I'm still in touch with some of those amazing young people.

Often when we serve others with no strings attached, we receive more than we give. These other people can help us without our even knowing it.

At the "Going Away" celebration for me at this youth center, Johnny, one of the center directors, said, "Wherever you go, you'll always have friends." And that has proven to be true.

MY COMMUNITY OF
FRIENDS, PEERS

Our community of friends can literally be a lifesaver for us. Earlier, I mentioned that I was depressed for nine months and didn't know it. Initially, Roger got me laughing like I hadn't laughed in months. Then, introducing Roger to David, my other friend, whom I often call my pastor, was special because they developed a special friendship. By my introducing them, my support group grew larger. We spent a couple of days together, and God used them to help me feel safe, accepted, and understood.

This time with this particular support group *saved* me when I didn't realize I needed saving. They brought me back so I could cope with myself and the stresses of my world. God used them to refresh me.

Today, David and I are still in a close friendship. God has given me other friends and peers: Jerald, another David, and Johnny. I serve on two boards, my own BLR and the Fatherhood CoMission. These boards provide more family-type relationships with accountability. I'm very fortunate to be in a group of professional writers, who call themselves "The Stinklings." They are brilliant men with whom I can discuss anything. However, all of us hold each other accountable for what we say. It is an affirming group.

Let your friends, if possible, be the ones with whom you can pray and spend time in the Bible. This can create a close community for you.

MY COMMUNITY OF ELDERS

With Dad dying when I was twenty years old, I didn't fully know what it meant to be a man. I found myself gravitating to older men, father figures. I knew that I could always call Gary Chapman, who is my spiritual dad. But we lived in different cities.

"Indirectly, helping others can lower our chances of depression."

If I met a man from whom I thought I could learn about life, I'd ask him to consider mentoring me. (I have since learned that this is unusual!)

I developed a twenty-three-year-father relationship with the late Bob Cook. Chicago pastor Donald Sharp has been like a father to me since 1994. After Bob Cook's death, Gordon Loux became a mentor. Dr. Bill Pannell, an author and retired seminary professor, is another one of my father figures. The late John Bass, a former nonprofit executive, invested in me.

I was also blessed to have women mentors as well. Karolyn Chapman mentored me every time she made me breakfast when I was in town and gave me her words of wisdom. The late Rushsella

Latimer helped and encouraged me spiritually. Older girls in college, who wouldn't date me, helped me better understand young ladies. Brenda Smith mentored me when I reported directly to her while working on a megachurch staff. Most recently, Penny Kievet, former CEO and president of a non-profit, has become a mentor to me.

All of these godly and successful men and women focused on serving others in order to find fulfillment. Indirectly, helping others can lower our chances of depression because: (1) serving others is a temporary distraction from concentrating only on yourself; (2) serving others, especially our elders, will often give us time-tested wisdom for living life; (3) this interaction with older and life-experienced adults can also provide hope, possibly counteracting, to some extent, depression; and (4) helping others makes you feel good!

IF YOU DON'T HAVE A COMMUNITY

SPEND TIME APPRECIATING NATURE

I'm so fortunate to live in Colorado Springs. Every day, I have the privilege of seeing Pike's Peak. Initially, I thought that at some point in time, I would get tired of looking at this beautiful mountain. But I have never in nearly thirty years grown tired of viewing it. Why?

My first look at this majestic mountain just made me feel good. Then I discovered that looking at this mountain gave me hope even during my most difficult days. When I remember that God made the earth for me and that even this beautiful mountain is for me, it makes me think that God, the creator of everything, loves me more than this mountain! My thoughts continue that if God can make something this big and majestic, then he can handle my problems! Thus, the mountains, the rivers, streams, the sky, the stars—all of nature have become a source of hope for me. This hope in just seeing some of the power of God on display causes my depression to retreat. Often my depression will disappear entirely, or at least lessen.

Psalm 19:1–2 reads, "The heavens proclaim the glory of God. The skies display his craftmanship. Day after day they continue to speak [to our soul]; night after night they make him known." They speak without words. Nature communicates with our spirit.

ANOTHER NON-COMMUNITY OPTION

A literal step you can take is to begin to take a walk each day or a few times a week. For me, exercise has become another source of mental distraction from my depression. Exercise is good for you. One of its benefits is that after the exercise, most people feel better physically and mentally. Science shows that exercise releases endorphins that combat depression.

I play tennis, lift weights, and swim. While practicing these activities, I usually meet people. It can begin with a smile or a positive nod of the head. We start unassuming conversations and, sometimes, you make an acquaintance who may become a friend later. You just never know.

IF NATURE OR EXERCISE
DOESN'T WORK FOR YOU

Other than looking at nature and exercising, what is another option if you don't have a community?

In my singles book *Single and Free to Be Me*, I suggest that you can try to create your own support group by just being friendly to others, especially by seeking to help an elderly person. Consider trying to find someone to help who can't help you in return.

Ask God to bring people to you to be your friends, who will love you enough to tell you what you need to hear, even when you don't want to hear it.

Maybe you are thinking, *I'm too afraid to ask people.* I totally get it. But look at it this way: by taking a chance, you may make a new friend. If you don't, then nothing changes.

Take a chance. You are worth it!

DR. MO'S COUCH

I will not belabor or repeat what I've stated in the previous chapter about churches and small groups. I love the suggestions Clarence has given. I have already warned about the factors that must be taken into consideration.

"Community" is such the buzzword these days. In some ways, it can feel like one more thing a person does not have or cannot obtain. I am hopeful you will embrace Clarence's encouragement that you are worth it! However, I do understand some obstacles, big or small, can be present and seem to be insurmountable.

When you are in a dark place, sometimes it can feel overwhelming to be a part of a community. Although you are hearing of the safety and healing experienced and found in community, it can still feel very frightening and uncertain. And that's simply okay. Your lived experiences may include some pretty horrific and traumatic events. Your pace might not be the same as another's pace. However long or short your strides may be, you are still moving. And that's the most important thing to keep in mind.

For some, it just does not feel safe to be around others. And this can even be with a supportive family. And then there are those who do not have supportive families. To whom do you turn and look to for support when your own family is the source of your pain or trauma?

Maybe you never realized your family is already a community. If you can depend on your family as a system of support, then, by all means, share with them how you need their support. Or consider holding a family meeting where everyone can discuss what he or she needs from the familial community. The family can discuss ways each member can be supported and championed. Also, you can discuss ways to keep the family healthy for every member. This can include calling special meetings when a member is having a difficult time. Or to inform a family member of an offense, whether intended or incidental. And do not forget to rejoice when others rejoice (as stated in 1 Corinthians 12:26) by coming together to celebrate special occasions and accomplishments.

Families have to be very intentional to establish a safe community for not only the members, but also those who are outside of the family. There may be neighbors or friends or extended family members or church members who might need to seek support in your family.

And if you do not or did not have a supportive family community, and you do not know where to turn, I will offer some suggestions. Because the question has been asked: Where do you turn?

Clarence laid out some beautiful reminders about God and some suggestions that are non-community options. These hopefully can feel less overwhelming and more doable. I feel for those who unfortunately have experienced God being wielded as a weapon and not as a Father who loves and chastises out of love. And for those who prefer to worship God in creation. These are helpful ways to create community. And I hope these aid in your exercising more courage to engage in the other examples of community Clarence has already mentioned.

God is a community by himself. When God said in Genesis 1:26, "Let *us* make man in *our* image" (KJV, emphasis mine), this shows God in relationship with himself. He is the Godhead. The Trinity. Consisting of the Father, the Son, and the Holy Spirit (Matthew 28:19). When we lean into the person of God and recognize how we can engage with the various roles of the Godhead, we enter into conscious relationship. We become more aware of God the Father or God as Creator, as Clarence mentioned when he gazes upon the majestic mountainous views.

The beach is one of the best places for me when I need *that* kind of communing with God. Every time I gaze upon the ocean and realize that I cannot see the end from where I stand, God speaks. I am reminded he is *vast*. In every way imaginable, he is *bigger*. And *deeper*. When I think about the depths one must go to remotely come near the ocean's floor, it again reminds me that God is beyond what I can even think. And there is more to him and more than the eyes can see. And his ways are limitless. You cannot bottom out when it comes to who God is and what he can do.

God is bigger than the darkest of our experiences. His Son is our co-heir. He died for your sins so that you would not have to endure as he did. He makes intercession for you now. He *still* relates to you. And the Holy Spirit is living within you. You have a community right at your disposal! What a blessing!

I am hopeful and prayerful that the community you have with God empowers you to do more community among those with whom you dwell. God himself declared, "It is not good for man to be alone," in Genesis 2:18 (DRB). May you find others with whom you can rule *together*. Especially over darkness and the agents thereof.

Another suggestion I want to bring to mind is for you to develop the intrapersonal relationship. That means the relationship with yourself. It can seem awkward to think of focusing on this relationship with self. However, the bedrock of any other relationship is dependent upon this relationship with self. So it stands to reason that healthy relationships are dependent upon a healthy relationship with self. Not perfect. Healthy.

So when you have been in a dark place, you might not feel so great about yourself. Clarence has discussed numerous dark places. You can feel less about yourself due to your adverse childhood experiences. Because other people do not value you or treat you fairly. Because you are suffering from illness. Or depression.

As I have stated throughout the book, there are times you might need to seek out a professional counselor. As you are seeking to establish community, and if it is so difficult that it might become immobilizing, please seek out a professional therapist.

Going to counseling can help you in a safe and trusted environment establish the work of developing or strengthening your intrapersonal relationship. Places where you have lost touch with yourself. Places where you do not trust yourself. Places where you have been made to doubt yourself. Places where you carry burdens that were placed on you. Places where there is shame for the sins others perpetrated against you.

Once you begin the work of seeing yourself as God created you, there is an increased likelihood you are willing to engage in community with others. And your counselor can help guide you through that process of moving toward community with others. Because, again, I do not want to assume that it's easy to move toward others. There are too many lived experiences of some that do not render this to be an easy solution. It can definitely be a corrective, emotional experience when the proper boundaries are in place. And when people are as much others-aware as they are self-aware, they can be conduits for a powerfully healing experience within a community.

You do not always have to seek counseling to develop that intrapersonal relationship. It can be as Clarence suggested. When you engage in exercise, you are giving space for yourself to engage in self-care. You are making yourself a priority. You are saying, "I am worth this investment in myself."

Spend time doing things or discovering things that make you happy. Try a new hobby. Read a book. Take a trip. Explore your creative side. Get to know who you are instead of the person you have been for everyone else. Which usually is at your expense.

Finally, altruism is always positive. To Clarence's point, help someone who can do nothing for you. Doing things for others who are really in no position to do anything for you or to you (for the most part) can be beneficial to your being. It makes you feel good to do good things for others. Sometimes this is a less risky way to *be* with others before you get involved *with* others. And it can be a way to be the change you wish you had in your life. Creating a community for those whom you can care for in ways that you desired to have automatically places you in community. How beautiful is that!

YOUR JOURNEY

Although you are hearing of the safety and healing experienced and found in community, it can still feel very frightening and uncertain. And that's simply okay. Your lived experiences may include some pretty horrific and traumatic events. Your pace might not be the same as another's pace. However long or short your strides may be, you are still moving.

- How does being in a small group or some kind of community sound to you?

- Have you ever been in a small group or some type of community? What was your experience?

- How does nature affect you?

- If you don't exercise or walk, would you consider starting? What would you choose to do if you were going to begin to exercise?

How does the idea of starting your own community grab you? I realize this may not be possible for you. But if you were going to be friendly to someone in your neighborhood, who would it be and why?

1. _____
   _____

2. _____
   _____

3. _____
   _____

Is the possibility of having another person in your life worth taking a baby step to begin the process?

CHAPTER FOURTEEN

EVERY DAY CAN BE YOUR BEST DAY

Dr. Gary Chapman has a saying: "We should live every day as though it is our last day, and then, every day can be our best day." Processing Dr. Chapman's saying led me to some conclusions. If we live each day as our last, there are certain things we'll want to get done:

- We will not want our last day to be lived with any regrets.

- We won't procrastinate.

- We will try to make sure all our relationships are healthy as much as is humanly possible. This would include asking for forgiveness or granting forgiveness, especially for immediate family and relatives. Such actions would provide us with peace of mind.

- We will not want to be in any debt that our family might have to repay. We will want to make sure that our family is taken care of emotionally and financially should something unexpected happen to us. For example, I write books. So I should do my best to make sure I completed my last book in order for my family to benefit from its book sales.

- We should make an effort to be especially kind with our words.

- We would probably be more patient with people, especially family.

- We would probably be better drivers. For example, I let people in the space in front of me instead of speeding up to make sure they couldn't get in front of me.

- Maybe if you are a people-pleaser to the detriment of yourself, you can in a nice way be less of a people-pleaser and be truer to yourself. Don't violate your conscience trying to please others.

- Also, very close to being a people pleaser, some people violate their conscience.

- Maybe we put things in order so that if we should die this day, things like our plans for our funeral service and will are in place, not leaving it on the family to try to figure it out.

"But we have the choice to let those issues stress us or use them to bless others and keep ourselves free from stress."

You get the idea. What would you add to this list?

A possible purpose behind Dr. Chapman's quote is that all of the issues on the list can create stress and/or depress us.

But we have the choice to let those issues stress us or use them to bless others and keep ourselves free from stress. For example, when we are driving and another driver is trying to beat us to a spot in order to get in front of us, why not choose to let them go first?

The other driver may wave their hand to thank us or may not. But we were in control. We chose to let them in. Thus, we are not stressing about the other driver being so rude to race to get in front of us. This is one less issue to fret and stress us. We are no longer carrying such an unimportant matter with us the rest of the day, wanting justice. Simple and doable. What do you think?

LIVING LIFE TO THE FULLEST

To live our lives to the fullest, then, it seems to be essential that we try to make our dreams a reality. In some ways, I believe our dreams energize us and give us purpose. Trying to live out our dreams seems to make life so much fun, even if we are not successful. We can always feel so good about ourselves because we tried. So we may need to convince ourselves once in a while to take a risk.

Our risk could be asking someone out on a date. If that person says "No," at least we asked. They missed out on meeting us, and we are worth getting to know—everyone is! Maybe it is trying out for a team. If we don't make it this year, at least we now know what is required. We can decide if we want to try out again next year or not. But we are in control of ourselves. Maybe it is a job interview. If we don't get the job, we may learn some crucial lessons during the interview that could help us on our next job interview. Again, we are in control.

Unfortunately, some of us, even with our dreams, imprison ourselves with a negative attitude. Our negative attitude filters every aspect of our lives. For those of us who feel this way, we always assume that our best isn't and never will be good enough. Therefore, we are afraid to try because we think we'll only get rejected.

Somehow, this kind of thinking makes some of us definitely feel safe; we are never going to be rejected or fail in a situation because we don't try. But this way of living isn't painless because we long to have our dream become reality. We can become subconsciously an incredibly negative person to be around because we are frustrated with ourselves for not trying. And we can never succeed with this attitude. We unintentionally dump our frustration on those with whom we are close because those who don't love us will not tolerate our behavior.

Take a shot at emotional freedom by taking a risk! You can do it. For some of us, our success will be in trying.

BECOME OTHER-PEOPLE FOCUSED

Another thought in learning to live each day as though it is your last day is becoming other-people focused. All the amazing men and women who have invested in my life were and are other-people focused.

I'm not suggesting doing big things for people like buying everyone we know a birthday or Christmas gift. That might actually increase our stress and theirs because now they feel obligated to give us a birthday or Christmas gift.

Consider being polite in stressful situations, for example, when you're at the airport. Being polite with the reservationist will bless him or her and might also bless us. Too often airline personnel, who have nothing to do with our flights being delayed or canceled, get verbally abused. But if we are patient, our attitude can take some of the stress off of them as they are trying to help us. Sometimes I will say to the reservationist, "It's not your fault." I've seen airline personnel's eyes light up hearing these words. And often that person will go the extra mile for me after I've been sensitive to them.

We can be polite. In the South, we say "Hey" to people whether we know them or not. This is a strange occurrence to New Yorkers and people in big cities in the North. If you are in the North, most times you probably don't focus on making eye contact with people. It can be seen as an invasion of privacy and, in some cases, could be dangerous.

But in an airport or in a store, there could be times in which we could say "Hello" or something appropriate for the situation. For example, on a plane, I will often say to the person seated beside me, "How are you doing today?" This is a tremendous stress reliever for a flyer who barely made the flight or has been stuck in the airport due to weather or mechanical delays. Such a question allows that person to vent. Your kindness blesses someone who needed to vent.

Maybe in a store, a person drops something or knocks something over. We can pick it up and put it back where it belongs and give a smile that says, "I've done that before myself."

In Genesis, the first book in the Bible, Joseph was a teenager and his father's favorite son. His brothers sold him into slavery. To make matters worse, Joseph was accused of a rape that he didn't commit and was put in prison. While he was in prison, two other prisoners asked for help. Joseph was able to help them. Later, one of the men he helped was able to help Joseph get out of prison.

When we help others while we are suffering, it often takes our mind momentarily off of our troubles. And helping others usually makes us feel good about helping someone in need. It also makes us feel good about ourselves.

So consider living each day as though it is your last day and see how it works for you. See if it lowers your stress and see if you are depressed less. If it doesn't help, at least you helped someone who may have desperately needed your brief friendship when he or she was in a stressful situation.

DR. MO'S COUCH

I hope since you have made it to this place in the book, you will choose to live as though it is your last day, and not plan to make it your last day. It can seem overwhelming to live each day as our last if we've been in a dark place for quite some time. How might we go from being in a dark place, maybe at times wishing it were our last day, to living with purpose as though it could be our last day?

Clarence has indeed given some very practical ways that do not require too much energy. However, if his suggestions still feel a bit overwhelming, take the focus off of making it your best day. Just start implementing the small choices he suggests: a kind word here, a smile there, or a helping hand. Altruism has been associated with having positive effects on an individual's emotional, mental, and spiritual well-being. So it is good to shift the focus to others.

However, I caution us to make sure our shift to focusing on others doesn't serve to distract from our work. We have to make certain that we continue to attend to those feelings that are usually associated with being in a dark place. Continue therapy. Continue exercising. Continue pursuing healthy eating options. Continue to take meds if prescribed. Continue all those things we realize have been beneficial during this time.

It is helpful to our overall well-being when we do think of others and focus on them. It becomes problematic when we use it as a means of deflection to never sit with (and in) the dark place. Think of it as a sort of rehabilitation. With physical therapy, we go in a few times a week or month for focused and intensive work on whatever part needs to be rehabilitated. The physical therapist might suggest doing a few of the techniques at home in between appointments. Typically, we leave rehab, and we are done with that work. Again, we might reinforce from time to time, but we do not spend all of the time outside of rehab doing what we do in rehab.

Such it is with our lives. Outside of the times of "rehab," we are employing these suggestions that Clarence has given us to make every day as though it is or will be our best day. We just need to be mindful that it doesn't negate the continued work of attending to the effects of the dark place.

I think sometimes it is easier to look in retrospect. After we have taken baby steps to allow ourselves to dream again, to allow ourselves to imagine some "best" days, it may be easier to start the day with that focus in mind. *Today will be the best day of my life.* However, if that feels too daunting, you can reflect when the day is done. Sometimes it is okay, when settling down for the evening or night, to review what was accomplished in that given day. It is okay to then determine there have been some good elements to the day. Eventually, we may be able to determine, *This was one of my best days.* We may be able to say that tomorrow will be a best day too.

Baby steps. Take the dreams. And do one thing, then the next. Don't worry about whether it will become "true" or not. We don't want to self-sabotage an operation. Just take little steps. Take the day. Make the best choice in the moment.

Transformation is not always a dramatic process, but little by little. It is not as radical as the "before's" and "after's" in extreme makeovers for homes, beauty, or weight loss. Usually it is the day-by-day, step-by-step process of shifting the mindset, just a hair to the left or right. It's not like moving a mountain, just a subtle shift. Over time, minds are renewed. The shift is then the norm. And before we know it, we are transformed. And maybe, just maybe, we can *then* say that these days have been some of the best days of our lives.

YOUR JOURNEY

When we help others while we are suffering, it often takes our mind momentarily off of our troubles. And helping others usually makes us feel good about helping someone in need. It also makes us feel good about ourselves. So consider living each day as though it is your last day and see how it works for you.

- What do you think about the possibility that every day can be your best day?

- What did you add to the list in regard to living each day as though it is your last day? Why did you add what you did?

What are your dreams?

1. _____

_____

2. _____

_____

3. _____

_____

- Which one of your dreams will you try to make a reality?

- For one week, if you are not already doing this, try being other-people focused. Start with your family. They might go into shock, but they will get over it.

FINAL WORDS FROM CLARENCE

My prayer is that this book has been and will continue to be a blessing and resource for you and possibly for your family and friends as you refer to it and practice its principles.

Most of all, as you read this book, hopefully you felt the love coming from God, Dr. Mo, and me for you and your well-being. Our goal was to be sensitive to you because some of you may be in a fragile condition. So we tried to find a balance of gently encouraging you regarding possible choices for yourself without putting pressure on you. Our desire was to caringly assist you to face your fear and possibly experience that what you feared was not as bad as you feared.

It still blows me away, knowing that God is with me whenever I enter a dark place. Additionally, he has riches and treasures in that dark place. Most important to me is that he is the one who heals me in this dark place, so I don't have to rush to get out of it before I'm healed. Thus, my dark place can be a sacred place if I'm listening to God's voice and following his direction. All of this can be true for you too if you will trust God. God is always with those of us who invite him into their lives. God will never force himself on you.

Usually when God heals us spiritually, he also teaches us, which leads to a deeper level of intimacy with him. God is so concerned about our emotional well-being.

It is Dr. Mo's and my hope that you now have a better understanding of how God sees, loves, and empowers you. With this understanding, we hope that you now know, if you didn't before, that you actually have choices that can impact you positively emotionally.

You were exposed to a lot of tools to help you, too.

So how am I dealing with my depression? Well, after coming out of my dark place, I have several takeaways. They have helped me. Maybe they can help you.

- I don't take myself quite as seriously as I used to.

- I put less pressure on myself. I don't have to be "It" or "The Best."

- I'm learning to do my best and leave the results to God—knowing the results don't define me.

- I'm learning to rest physically, emotionally (making wise choices), and spiritually—letting God lead me.

- I'm more patient with myself and difficult situations.

- Amazingly, I'm more patient with people than I used to be. I think this is because I realize that I have my own issues and that I'm far from perfect.

- I'm listening to God more through his word (the Bible), the Holy Spirit, my wife, my daughters, my spiritual sons, and Christ-honoring music.

After I came out of my depression, God began opening amazing ministry doors—actually pretty much everything I thought I wanted and needed. God has shown me that those "ministry things" are fun. But it is really all about the peace God gives me as I'm learning to trust him more and more. So for me, instead of trying to compete with other Christians for notoriety, I'm content to wait for God to do what he wants to do for me, to me, and through me.

God can now let me experience more ministry opportunities on a larger platform because I know that those opportunities and experiences don't define me. I'm just there to help others. These events are no longer idols for me.

This is my new priority: Most people want to be loved. Most people respond to Jesus Christ's love. So I try to love people with his love with no agenda.

This is my new mindset. It has taken so much stress off my shoulders. Maybe it will work for you, too.

You read Christina's poem earlier in the book. I wonder if it provides you with more hope now that you have read this book?

"Shell of an Animal"

Most people see my shell, as I use it to protect me.
I may use my shell to blend in or to be left alone.
Sometimes, I will use it as I reveal hints of myself.
I use my shell to hide my anger, pain, and fear.
In safety, my animal will emerge.

So remember, the next time (if there is a next time) you find yourself in a dark place, now you know what to do. Blessings!

NEVER BE ALONE AGAIN

I wrote this book with you in mind because I want the very best for you by providing an opportunity for you to experience the very best life has to offer.

The best way I've found to experience life's best has been through my personal relationship with Jesus Christ. In chapter nine, I shared that I contemplated death by suicide before I had a personal relationship with Jesus. My relationship with Jesus Christ keeps me from ever being completely alone.

Remember my panic attack situation? Do you remember what helped me to overcome my panic? It was my personal relationship with Jesus Christ. Remember how the Christian music I listened to that morning calmed my soul because it reminded me of Jesus's love for me.

If you don't know Jesus Christ, let me introduce you to him. Here are some facts that you need to understand before you can establish a relationship with Jesus.

The first fact is that God the Father created the earth as well as Adam and Eve, the first humans from which all humans come. God made everything for them and placed them in the Garden of Eden. He only had one rule—that they wouldn't eat from the tree of knowledge of good and evil. The consequence of eating from the tree was death. Adam and Eve disobeyed (often called sin) God and ate from that tree.

But God didn't kill them. He banished them from the Garden of Eden. God made plans to sacrifice his only Son, Jesus, to pay for Adam and Eve's disobedience. In chapter 2 verses 14–15 of Hebrews, one of the books in the Bible—God's love letter to us—it states, "Because God's children are human beings—made of flesh and blood—the Son (Jesus) also became flesh and blood. For only as a human being could he die, and by dying could he break the power of the devil, who had the power of death. Only in this way could he set free all who have lived their lives as slaves to the fear of dying."

Hebrews 9:14b reads, "For by the power of the eternal Spirit, Christ offered himself to God as a perfect sacrifice for our sins." And in the same chapter, verse 22 says, "In fact, according to the law of Moses, nearly everything was purified with blood. For without the shedding of blood, there is no forgiveness."

What is sin? Sin is to disobey God. It also means to do your very best and still fall short of God's standard. Imagine being on a basketball team. Your team is down one point with two seconds left. It's your team's ball. Your coach tells you to take the last shot! You take the shot but miss and your team loses. With God it is not us trying to live a good life, hoping our good outweighs our bad. Due to Adam and Eve's disobedience, all humans are born with a nature to do bad.

To rescue us, Jesus dies in our place to pay the penalty of our sin. Hebrews 9:15b states, "For Christ died to set them free from the penalty of the sins they had committed under that first covenant."

If you would like a personal relationship with Jesus Christ, Hebrews 11:6 says, "And it is impossible to please God without faith. Anyone who wants to come to him must believe that God exists and that he rewards those who sincerely seek him."

What is faith? Hebrews 11:1 defines faith as "the confidence that what we hope for will actually happen. It gives us assurance about things we cannot see."

To have a personal relationship with Jesus Christ, you must believe what the following verses say. Romans 3:23 says, "For everyone has sinned; we all fall short of God's glorious standard." Romans 6:23 explains, "For the wages of sin is death, but the free gift of God is eternal life through Jesus Christ our Lord." Romans 5:8 emphasizes, "But

God showed his great love for us by sending Christ to die for us while we were still sinners."

This is what you must do to accept Jesus Christ as your Savior—it is in Romans 10:9–10, "If you confess with your mouth that Jesus is Lord and believe in your heart that God raised him from the dead, you will be saved. For it is by believing in your heart that you are made right with God, and it is by confessing with your mouth that you are saved."

To know Jesus, you simply ask God to forgive you for your sins and to come into your heart and for him to make your life what he wants it to be.

Here's a prayer you can pray. The words aren't magic. If you believe what you are saying, Jesus will come into your life:

God, thank you for sending your Son, Jesus, to die on the cross for my sins. I recognize that I've been trying to make life work without you. Please forgive me. I receive you as my Savior and Lord. Thank you for forgiving me of my sins and giving me eternal life. Help me to love you with all that I am and have and from this point forward and to love those around me like you love me.

ACKNOWLEDGMENTS

Special thanks to Dr. Monique Gadson, my counselor, who God used to help me better understand myself and my depression. She helped me to understand that working through my dark place is not necessarily about getting over it. And that I don't have to rush out of my dark place. Dr. Gadson introduced me to the idea that my dark place can be a holy place. That thought was so profound for me.

Thanks to Greg Johnson, my literary agent. After he heard about the responses of those who heard me speak about my depression, he encouraged me to write this book. Finally and reluctantly, I did. Without Greg, this book never gets written.

I'm so grateful to Amy Roemer, Jenee Hamilton, Berry Huffman, Stan and Debbie Senft, and the Stinklings for all of your editorial assistance.

Most of all, I'm so incredibly grateful for Brenda, my wife, who has patiently and graciously loved me and stayed with me when I'm in a dark place. Truly, she is a gift from God.

—*Clarence Shuler*

To Dr. Clarence Shuler, you are my friend and intercessor. You often call me your counselor. However, I have always been a concerned friend. I am so grateful you took heed to the gentle nudges to consider your emotional and mental well-being. Thank you for inviting me to coauthor and contribute to this sacred record of your lived experiences. What a tremendous honor and privilege!

Thank you, Brenda, for your grace and kindness. I appreciate how you bear witness as a godly wife and mother to girls.

Thank you—Jerome, Imani, and Nia—for being light when I find myself in dark places. I love each of you with everything in me.

To God be the glory for the things he has done!

—*Dr. Monique Gadson*

ENDNOTES

1. Alyssa Yeo, "The Story of Two Wolves," Urban Balance, February 24, 2016, https://www.urbanbalance.com/the-story-of-two-wolves/.

2. The last nine questions are from Gary Chapman and Clarence Shuler, *Choose Greatness: 11 Wise Decisions Brave Young Men Make* (Chicago: Northfield Publishing, 2019), 158. Used by permission.

3. Chuck Swindoll, "Contradictory Truths, Part Two," Insight for Living Ministries, November 7, 2017, https://www.insight.org/resources/daily-devotional/individual/contradictory-truths-part-two.

4. Viola Davis (@violadavis), "Cute Texts To Send Someone With Depression: When They Socially Withdraw," Instagram post, January 2, 2022, https://www.instagram.com/p/CYPqD5TP2GF/?utm_medium=copy_link.

5. Bishop Louis Greenup Jr., lecture delivered at T. D. Jakes' ManPower Conference, 1998.

6. Charmas B. Lee, Janice K. Lee, and Patricia L. Dennard, *Think Say Do: Disrupting Systemic Cycles of Faulty Thinking* (independently published, 2019), 24.

7. Madison Keys, quoted in D'Arcy Maine, "Australian Open 2022: Madison Keys and Jessica Pegula, Americans abroad, could meet, but first face daunting opponents," ESPN.com, January 24, 2022, https://www.espn.com/tennis/story/_/id/33135783/australian-open-2022-madison-keys-jessica-pegula-americans-abroad-meet-first-face-daunting-opponent.s.

8. Jerald January Sr., "When Dreams Become Reality, Part 6," Vernon Park Church of God, August 1, 2021, YouTube video, https://www.youtube.com/watch?v=jKaHAoFsR1Q&list=PL1R05Y2Hcu-uA6rjeSiuAcRPU8NDS-Fyyo&index=25.

9. This magazine is now called *Instigate*, sponsored by Citygate.

10. I heard this song after coming out of my depression and I highly recommend it.

11. Catherine H. Rogers, Frank J. Floyd, Marsha Mailick Seltzer, Jan Greenberg, and Jinkuk Hong, "Long-Term Effects of the Death of a Child on Parents' Adjustment in Midlife," Journal of Family Psychology 22, no. 2 (2008): 203–11. https://www.ncbi.nlm.nih.gov/pmc/articles/PMC2841012/.

12. Rogers, Floyd, Seltzer, Greenberg, and Hong, "Long-Term Effects."

13. Clarence Shuler, "Biblical Tips for When You're in a Dark Place," Calvary Worship Center, July 1, 2018, YouTube video, https://www.youtube.com/watch?v=g4u11qf7MN8.

14. Clarence Shuler, Single and Free to Be Me (Colorado Springs: Building Lasting Relationships Publishing House, 2013), 65–66.

15. Terence Real, I Don't Want to Talk About It: Overcoming the Secret Legacy of Male Depression (New York: Scribner, 1997).

16. Craig Groeschel, "When You Feel Like Growing Up," Life Church, May 23, 2021, YouTube video, https://www.youtube.com/watch?v=wITHAgusAuI.

17. Craig Groeschel, "When Life Feels Out of Control," Hope City, July 26, 2020, YouTube video, https://www.youtube.com/watch?v=GgTTe2 RekOs. Two of his other sermon titles are "Healing From Shame: Deep Clean" (Life Church, April 4, 2021, YouTube video, https://www.youtube.com/watch?v=2nC8rE1il2Y) and "When You Can't Take It Anymore" (Life Church, June 2, 2019, YouTube video, https://www.youtube.com/watch?v=mero2wod-Yo).

18. Quoted in Martin N. Davidson, "Know Thine Adversary: The Impact of Race on Styles of Dealing with Conflict," Sex Roles: A Journal of Research 45, nos. 5–6 (September 1, 2001): 259–76.

19. Pew Research Center, https://www.pewforum.org/religious-landscape -study/gender-composition/men/2022.

20. Shelia Wray Gregoire in her endorsement for David Murrow, Why Men Hate Going to Church (Nashville: Thomas Nelson, 2005).

21. For more information, contact Christian Stronghold Church; contact information available at https://christianstronghold.com/ministries.php.

22. For more information, visit the Calvary Revival Church website at https://crcglobal.org.

23. Holly Meyer, "What new LifeWay Research survey says about why young adults are dropping out of church," Tennessean, January 15, 2019, https://www.tennessean.com/story/news/religion/2019/01/15/lifeway-research-survey-says-young-adults-dropping-out-church/2550997002/.

24. Meyer, "Lifeway Research."

25. Meyer, "LifeWay Research."

26. Meyer, "LifeWay Research."

ABOUT THE AUTHORS

DR. CLARENCE SHULER
(A.K.A. DOCTOR LOVE)

Dr. Shuler is the president/CEO of BLR: Building Lasting Relationships. He has been married to Brenda for over 37 years. They have three adult daughters. They conduct marriage, men's, women's, and singles seminars internationally. Clarence filmed a session as a relationship expert for Oprah's *Love Goals* reality show (2020). He speaks to youth,

college students, and singles about friendships, dating, biblical sex, pornography, and sexting. God uses him to help couples gain victory over affairs. He also disciples married couples to help them grow closer to God and each other. In 2020, Clarence and Brenda were presented the "Speakers of the Year Award" at FamilyLife's Weekend to Remember Marriage Getaway. Dr. Gary Chapman and Dr. Shuler speak together at *The Five Love Languages, Date Night,* and *Life-Changing Cross-Cultural Friendships* events. Clarence's *Maximizing Difference* (diversity) training is in constant demand. Clarence is a popular keynote speaker. He also speaks for Iron Sharpen Iron events and occasionally is a chapel speaker for National Football League teams.

Dr. Shuler is author of 10 books, including *Life-Changing Cross-Cultural Friendships: How You Can Help Heal Racial Divides, One Relationship at a Time* (2022), which is coauthored with Dr. Chapman. Presently, Clarence serves on the boards of Fatherhood CoMission and One Challenge International.

Clarence and Brenda are veterans of the pastorate and Christian organizations. They reside in Colorado Springs, Colorado. For more information, visit www.clarenceshuler.com.

MONIQUE S. GADSON, PHD, LPC

Dr. Gadson is an assistant professor of counseling psychology at Seattle School of Theology and Psychology, licensed professional counselor, consulting therapist, and podcast host. She received her MS in Clinical Mental Health Counseling from Troy State University, MS

in Spirituality and Counseling from Richmont Graduate University, and PhD in Marriage and Family Therapy from Amridge University.

Dr. Gadson hosts the podcast *And the Church Said,"* where she discusses church and culture from a Christian counseling perspective, focusing on mental and emotional health and the Christian faith. Visit www.drmoniquesmithgadson.com.

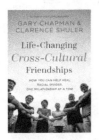

Other Books by Dr. Shuler (a.k.a. *The Love Doctor*):
Your Wife Can Be Your Best Friend
Keeping Your Wife Your Best Friend
Choose Greatness: Eleven Wise Decisions That Brave Young Men Make,
    coauthored with Dr. Gary Chapman
What All Dads Should Know, coauthored with Dr. Jeff Shears
Winning the Race to Unity: Is Racial Reconciliation Really Working?

FREE Relationship Video Series: *Common Mistakes Most Couples Make*,
visit www.clarenceshuler.com.

Book BLR's Relationship Seminars (719-282-1340):
The Marriage You've Always Wanted (facilitated by Clarence & Brenda)
Single and Free to Be Me
Understanding the Heart of a Man (women only)
What a Man Needs to Know About a Woman (men only)
Maximizing Difference (diversity training)

BLR's Mission Statement:
BLR gets wounded people into God's Word and God's Word in them,
healing, equipping, and empowering them to become reproductive
disciples, who do the same for others.

BLR Services:
BLR: Building Lasting Relationships is a faith-based organization that helps
couples experience thriving and lasting marriage relationships including
those in crisis. We encourage single adults regardless of their relationship
status, and assist youth to overcome pornography and sexting issues. We
also provide biblical diversity consulting and life coaching.

For more information or to contact Clarence Shuler, visit his
website at www.clarenceshuler.com.